Enigmas and Powers

Love to all

Princeton Theological Monograph Series

K. C. Hanson and Charles M. Collier, Series Editors

Recent volumes in the series:

Richard Valantasis et al., editors
The Subjective Eye: Essays in Honor of Margaret Miles

Anette Ejsing
A Theology of Anticipation: A Constructive Study of C. S. Peirce

Caryn Riswold
Coram Deo: Human Life in the Vision of God

Paul O. Ingram, editor
Constructing a Relational Cosmology

Michael G. Cartwright
*Practices, Politics, and Performance: Toward a Communal
Hermeneutic for Christian Ethics*

David A. Ackerman
*Lo, I Tell You a Mystery: Cross, Resurrection,
and Paraenesis in the Rhetoric of 1 Corinthians*

Lloyd Kim
*Polemic in the Book of Hebrews:
Anti-Judaism, Anti-Semitism, Supersessionism?*

Major Works by Walter Wink

John the Baptist in the Gospel Tradition
Cambridge University Press, 1968; reprinted, Wipf & Stock, 2000

The Bible in Human Transformation
Fortress Press, 1973

Transforming Bible Study
Abingdon, 1980; 2nd ed., 1990

Naming the Powers
Fortress Press, 1984

Unmasking the Powers
Fortress Press, 1986

Engaging the Powers
Fortress Press, 1992

Cracking the Gnostic Code
Scholars Press, 1993

When the Powers Fall
Fortress Press, 1998

The Powers That Be
Doubleday, 1998

The Human Being
Fortress Press, 2001

Jesus and Nonviolence
Fortress Press, 2003

Enigmas and Powers

Engaging the Work of Walter Wink
for Classroom, Church, and World

Edited by
D. Seiple *and*
Frederick W. Weidmann

PICKWICK *Publications* · Eugene, Oregon

ENIGMAS AND POWERS
Engaging the Work of Walter Wink for Classroom, Church, and World

Princeton Theological Monograph Series 79

ISBN 13: 978-1-55635-290-4

Cataloging-in-Publication data:

Enigmas and powers : engaging the work of Walter Wink for classroom, church, and world / edited by D. Seiple and Frederick W. Weidmann.

xxviii +140 p.; 23 cm. — Princeton Theological Monograph Series 79
Includes bibliographical references.

ISBN 13: 978-1-55635-290-4

1. Bible—Study and teaching. I. Wink, Walter. II. Seiple, D. III. Weidmann, Frederick W. IV. Title. V. Series.

BS600.2 E80 2008

To
Walter Wink and June Keener Wink
and to all who contribute
to our understanding and engagement
of the power of peace and justice

Contents

PART THREE: Enigmas of the Future

Contributors

Marcus Borg is Distinguished Professor of Religion and Culture at Oregon State University, Corvallis, Oregon.

Balfour Brickner, until his death in 2006, was Senior Rabbi Emeritus at Stephen Wise Free Synagogue and Executive Director of the Alfred and Gail Engelberg Foundation.

Tansy Chapman, one of the founders of the Bethany House of Prayer, Arlington Heights, Massachusetts, is an Episcopal priest.

Hal Childs is Executive Co-Director of the California Counseling Institute, San Francisco, California.

Bruce Chilton is Bernard Iddings Bell Professor of Religion, Chaplain of the College, and Executive Director of the Institute of Advanced Theology at Bard College, Annandale-on-Hudson, New York.

Richard Deats, until his retirement in 2005, served the Fellowship of Reconciliation in various capacities, including Executive Secretary, Director of Interfaith Activities, and Editor of *Fellowship* magazine.

J. Harold Ellens, founding editor-in-chief of the *Journal of Psychology and Christianity*, is a practicing psychotherapist and Presbyterian minister.

Robert (Bob) Evans is Senior Fellow at the Centre for Conflict Resolution in Cape Town, South Africa, and Executive Director of Plowshares Institute.

Ray Gingerich is Director of the Anabaptist Center for Religion and Society and Professor Emeritus of Theology and Ethics at Eastern Mennonite University, Harrisonburg, Virginia.

Ted Grimsrud is Associate Professor of Theology and Peace Studies at Eastern Mennonite University, Harrisonburg, Virginia.

Joseph C. Hough is President and William E. Dodge Professor of Social Ethics at Union Theological Seminary, New York, New York.

Amy-Jill Levine is E. Rhodes and Leona B. Carpenter Professor of New Testament Studies at Vanderbilt University, Nashville, Tennessee.

Alastair McIntosh is Visiting Professor of Human Ecology at the Centre for Human Ecology, University of Strathclyde, Scotland. Walter Wink describes his *Soil and Soul* as "a beautiful book, a fantastic book, a book that will help reconstitute the world."

Jack Miles, columnist and author, is Visiting Professor at Occidental College, Los Angeles, California, and Senior Fellow with the Pacific Council on International Policy.

Henry Mottu is Professor of Theology at the University of Geneva, Geneva, Switzerland.

Robert Raines is an ordained minister in the United Church of Christ and former Director of the Kirkridge Retreat and Study Center.

Sharon H. Ringe is Professor of New Testament at Wesley Theological Seminary, Washington, D.C.

Wayne G. Rollins is Adjunct Professor of Scripture at Hartford Seminary, Professor Emeritus of Theology at Assumption College, Worcester, Massachusetts, as well as Founder and Chair of the Society of Biblical Literature Section on Psychology and Biblical Studies.

Bonnie Rosborough is Pastor of the Briarcliff Congregational Church (UCC) in Briarcliff Manor, New York.

David Seiple is an independent scholar and minister affiliated with Broadway United Church of Christ, New York, New York.

Frederick W. Weidmann is Director of the Center for Church Life and Professor of Biblical Studies at Auburn Theological Seminary, New York, New York.

Barbara Wheeler is President and Director of the Center for the Study of Theological Education at Auburn Theological Seminary, New York, New York.

Bill Wylie-Kellerman is Director of Graduate Theological Urban Studies for SCUPE (Seminary Consortium for Urban Pastoral Education) in Chicago, Illinois.

Acknowledgements

A WORK LIKE THIS DOES NOT MAKE IT TO THE PRINTED PAGE WITH-
out the support, help and dedication of many colleagues. Our only fear
in listing them is that we will inadvertently leave someone out. Perhaps
there is a "third way." We will not pretend to be (capable of being)
exhaustive in our presentation of names, but rather exemplary. Behind
the important institutions and colleagues named herein, you can be sure
there are others. And they can be sure their efforts are worthwhile and
appreciated!

Walter Wink served for over three decades as Professor of Biblical
Interpretation at Auburn Theological Seminary in New York. This volume grows out of, and to a significant degree reflects, the "Celebration
of the Work of Walter Wink" held at Auburn Seminary in May 2005. To
design and organize such a program for any colleague is a challenge; to
do so for Walter Wink—given the breadth and depth of his work across
many disciplines, and across the divides too often experienced between
theory and practice, church and academy, and reflection and action—is
particularly challenging *and* important. Lee Hancock, then dean of
Auburn Seminary, did just that. Her contribution, in delineating the
many arenas and aspects of Walter's work, and in organizing esteemed
colleagues to speak to these, is felt in the particulars of this volume and
in the work as a whole.

Beyond the work of Dean Hancock and the festivities of the "celebration" in May 2005, Auburn Seminary has continued to support this
project in many ways, financial and otherwise. On matters of editing
and manuscript preparation, particularly in the final stages, thanks are
due to Letitia Campbell, formerly a program associate within Auburn's
Center for Church Life and currently a graduate student at Emory
University, for her input and expertise. On matters of logistical support
and advice, Lisa Anderson, education programs associate at Auburn, has

been a continual help in moving things along, as well as a source of good will and good humor. For their advice, overall support, and willingness to free up co-editor Fred Weidmann from some of his responsibilities at Auburn Seminary, particular thanks are due to Barbara Wheeler, president and Katharine Rhodes Henderson, executive vice president of Auburn Seminary.

On the publication side, it is not surprising, but nonetheless always gratifying, to work with good and creative colleagues. At Wipf and Stock, K. C. Hanson, editor-in-chief, knows—we hope—something of our gratitude for his receptivity and support in moving the work along to publication. Among many other colleagues who have had a hand in this project, Diane Farley, editorial assistant, has been especially helpful in keeping all things—including us—on track. Beyond Wipf and Stock, thanks are due also to colleagues at Fortress Press, publisher of several of Walter Wink's books, for their interest in this work and discussion and advice along the way; editor-in-chief Michael West, acquisitions editor Neil Elliot, and former editorial director Marshall Johnson have been particularly engaged and helpful.

A word of gratitude is due to the many contributors to this volume. We neither asked for nor received uniformity. Rather, we invited honest, robust, and creative engagement with the work of Walter Wink on the assumption that the legacy of that work is neither set nor settled. The contributors, in their own distinct voices, have provided examples, suggestions, and possibilities. We hope that you, the reader, will add your own expertise and efforts to their reflections. And we thank you ahead of time for the creative work that will follow.

A final word of thanks and gratitude to one whose own life's work showed the ways that make for peace, justice, and understanding. The reflection included in this volume was among the last formal presentations made by Rabbi Balfour Brickner—a widely respected and influential congregational leader, writer, teacher, and activist—before his death in August 2005. The printed word cannot take us back to that day in May 2005, or bring back the warmth, humor, and joy that Rabbi Brickner embodied. But it can reflect a little something of that spirit, even as it points us forward. We have dedicated this volume to Walter and June and to "all who contribute to our understanding and engage-

ment of the power of peace and justice." Surely among that number is
Rabbi Balfour Brickner, now of blessed memory.

D. Seiple
Frederick W. Weidmann
New York City
March 24, 2007
(Feast Day of Oscar Romero, bishop of El Salvador, martyr, 1980)

Introduction

by Frederick W. Weidmann

You hold in your hands an unusual book. In it you will find essays, letters, speeches, prayers, toasts, reminiscences, arguments, footnotes, and open-ended conversation. Put another way, you will find *addresses*: the authors are variously talking *to* God; the Spirit; Psyche; Walter Wink the person; Walter Wink the essay, book, theory, method, and/or argument(s); and finally, and throughout, to you, the reader. Most of all, you will find, I hope, truth—or at least meaningful, productive, and enticing movements toward truth, and toward the world in light of truth.

As a celebration of the ongoing work of the noted author, biblical scholar, peace activist, pastor, speaker, and workshop leader Walter Wink, along with his frequent collaborator June Keener Wink, this book is a Festschrift, to be sure. And, like the best of that genre, it is intended to celebrate and to amplify—perhaps even to advance—the named scholar's work. At the same time, however, this is a Festschrift that, like its honoree, seems incapable of sitting still.

Taken as a whole or even in its individual parts, what follows is not easily categorized or situated within accepted disciplinary categories. Nor does it presume a scholarly distance from the issues addressed, even when those issues are clearly scholarly. The editors and contributors to the volume attempt to reflect something of the depth and breadth of Walter Wink's output, influence, and potential. Yes, potential. For though any colleague would envy Walter's production and impact, and no colleague or student would require more, it is nonetheless the case that more is required by and for the institutions and communities—and, indeed, the principalities and powers—which Wink's work addresses. We hope that this collection suggests for individual readers and communities what and how that "more" might be, and how they might contribute.

∾

It is not a simple matter to describe or quantify Walter Wink's career, his place in the history of biblical scholarship, his influence on the practice of teaching, his impact on peace activism, or his understanding, more broadly, of God, humanity, the self, community, and the cosmos. Several essays in this volume focus on his publications, which are vast and impressive. But even here, one finds quick summaries impossible.

Wink's publications have addressed major issues recognized within the discipline of biblical studies, as well as major shortcomings of the discipline itself, previously unrecognized or denied. The *Powers* trilogy, beginning with *Naming the Powers: The Language of Power in the New Testament* (1984), defined, delineated, quantified, and qualified the presence of "power" in its various semantic, historic, psychological, and spiritual guises in ways never before attempted, let alone achieved, within New Testament scholarship. Wink's findings and their applications have had a clear and direct influence on the language and methods of the discipline.

At the same time, Wink and his findings have had a direct influence *outside* the discipline of biblical studies as scholars, practitioners, and others apply his work to their own endeavors. This expanding influence has been marked by further publications such as *The Powers that Be: Theology for a New Millennium* (1998), which serves as summary and (re)application of the material in the *Powers* trilogy, particularly its third and final volume.

And so it is with Wink's more recent, *The Human Being: Jesus and the Enigma of the Son of the Man* (2002). Like the *Powers* trilogy, it engages a complicated, little understood, and crucial problem within the field of New Testament studies. It breaks new ground using a range of methods, some tried and true, others new and suspect. It has already, happily, gained a wide reading both within and beyond the pale of biblical scholarship. At the same time, Walter tells me he is working on a new volume that will further develop this theme and make it accessible to a broader audience.

And then there are the books that, though fed by Walter's unique and probing biblical scholarship, are written purposely for those outside of the guild of New Testament studies. Perhaps atop that list would be *Jesus' Third Way: The Relevance of Non-Violence in South Africa Today* (1988), a book that has been crucial to the churches involved in the struggle to end Apartheid and shape the new South Africa. Several essays in this collection reflect on this important book. What goes around comes around. And so Walter's more recent, and related, work, *Jesus and Non-Violence: A Third Way* (2003), finds its audience not among practitioners *per se*, but back within the walls of academe, as Marcus Borg notes in his contribution here.

Sitting right atop the wall—or, better, breaking through the wall—of theory and practice are Walter's well known works on Bible study: *The Bible in Human Transformation: Toward a New Paradigm for Biblical Study* (1973), and *Transforming Bible Study: A Leader's Guide* (1980). While formulating critiques of, and prescribing correctives to, methods of biblical study which had long been accepted, and even unquestioned, within the guild, these works modeled and promoted approaches to scripture—and to self, community and environment—which have had direct influence far beyond the guild of professional bible scholars and their students in seminaries and universities.

∾

How might that influence be described? What is its mark, whether within the academy or outside? What is characteristically Winkian about Wink's work, wherever and however directed and applied?

Near the beginning of his *Powers that Be*, Wink writes, "I have seen enough of God's wily ways with the Powers to stake my life on the side of hope."[1] That sentence is useful in capturing something of the complicated essence and infectious drive of Wink's work. Notice that God and the Powers are taken seriously and seriously summoned in ways that make meaning. Notice too that "hope" comes last; that is, it has the last say. None of this simplistic analysis is meant to suggest naïveté. Quite the opposite. A very complex and often minutely described and argued framework of meaning permeates Wink's work. That meaning seriously engages both God and (often unrecognized) Powers, and it does so in ways that make sense for the texts and contexts under scrutiny *and* for the student of those texts and contexts. Further, however "objective" and "historical" the basis for Wink's arguments, propositions, and constructs, his analysis always, finally, suggests and promotes hope.

Second, and not unrelated to that profound call to hope, is a nod to, of all things, fear. First in *Engaging the Powers: Discernment and*

1. Wink, *The Powers that Be*, 10.

Resistance in a World of Domination (1992), and then in *The Powers that Be,* Wink writes provocatively, "What guilt was for Martin Luther, fear has become for us: the goad that can drive us to God."[2] As a Lutheran myself, I feel somewhat guilty in taking Wink's bait, but here we go. I would suggest that Wink has, in a deceptively simple recasting (or co-opting or overturning) of a central Lutheran tenet, identified something crucial to faithful living and, arguably, the acceptance of grace in our time. Fear drives what we do, as individuals, as communities, as nations, to an astounding and often unacknowledged degree. Simply recognizing this might make room for hope and evoke grace. Regardless, the diagnosis and its challenge are reflective of much of Wink's work as it appropriates a deep and meaningful tradition and calls us to our more authentic individual and collective selves.

A third characteristic that drives Wink's work, I suggest, is summarized in an aphorism from *Naming the Powers*: "It is a virtue to disbelieve what does not exist. It is dangerous to disbelieve what exists outside our current limited categories."[3] This statement marvelously straddles, and points beyond, the objectivism and positivism that continue to mark so much of the scholarly enterprise, as well as the strategies and tactics of individuals and communities engaged in various justice struggles around the world. Who would argue the first sentence? Ah, but who would entertain the second? And if so, when and how? With Wink's prodding, and supported by his characteristically thorough and persuasive analyses, many who might otherwise continue to ply their craft with willful, unknowing ignorance have been gracefully forced to reconsider the limits of the categories with which they have worked. Both scholars and activists will admit to this, at least in their more gracious and truthful moments.

Closely related to the previous characteristic is a fourth that can likewise be described with a quote found in *Naming the Powers*; this one, however, not from Wink himself, but from Michel Foucault. Wink writes: "I am, in short, trying to reconnoiter what Michel Foucault called the 'epistemological space specific to a particular period.'"[4] And so, Wink embarks on his project to un-demythologize—to remytholo-

2. Ibid., 161. In *Engaging the Powers*, the exact statement is, "What guilt was for Luther, the enemy has become for us: the goad that can drive us to God" (263).

3. Wink, *Naming the Powers*, 4.

4. Ibid., 7.

gize, or reappropriate, or "transpose. . .into a new key"—that New Testament myth which falls flat and loses its meaning, both within itself and for us, *apart* from any reference to the principalities and powers Wink describes.[5] As Wink clearly shows, given the "epistemological space" of meaning *then*—that is, at the time the biblical texts were written—one cannot presume *now* to demythologize the powers with full integrity; their *full* meaning is inevitably lost to us. That said, given the "epistemological space" available within the guild of biblical scholarship at the time when Wink was working, one could not have presumed to interpret those references or engage those powers in *any* meaningful way.

In constructing a meaningful scholarly framework for engaging the powers, Wink was forced to (re)create or (re)construct "epistemological space" for *this* period and for *this* context. Using Peter Berger's *Sacred Canopy* as a foil, Wink showed how broadly accepted scholarly assumptions had themselves become "incompetent to judge" the task at hand.[6] Analogously, in carrying out his work on and with the powers beyond the scholarly pale, Wink was compelled to clear "space" for applying and, better, adapting Jesus' "third way." And, of course, that work continues through the publication of *The Human Being* and beyond.

Finally, in this very brief overview of Wink's work and influence, it is perhaps appropriate that the parting nod should go not to any given element or characteristic of Wink's work *per se*. What do I mean? In a footnote within *Naming the Powers*, in a passing consideration of "this 'postmodern' worldview" fostered by the new physics, Wink writes, "It is not so much the 'new physics' itself that is of value here (although it is a great help) as it is the new situation of openness and flux that it makes possible."[7] Though I would not soon write off the continuing and lasting value of Wink's own work, and therefore have no interest in drawing too tight an analogy, I do suggest that one sure mark of Wink's work is the "openness and flux that it makes possible."

Clearly this is so for both his continued exposition and his application of Jesus' third way. As Wink writes of three pericopes from the Sermon on the Mount (turning the other cheek; giving up the garment;

5. Ibid., 6, 104.
6. Ibid., 102; Berger, *The Sacred Canopy*.
7. Wink, *Naming the Powers*, 104 n. 1.

and walking the second mile) that serve as the basis of the "third way": "These are, of course, not rules to be followed legalistically, but examples to spark an infinite variety of creative responses in new and changing circumstances."[8] A similar assertion might be made for Wink's work as a whole—again, whether intended primarily for academics, practitioners, or some combination thereof: by breaking down barriers, by providing the strong and necessary arguments, by suggesting avenues for moving forward, Wink's work opens up new and promising horizons for exploration, application, and action.

∽

To mark the retirement of Walter Wink from the position of Professor of Biblical Interpretation at Auburn Theological Seminary in New York in May 2005, the Seminary deigned to throw a party. Or so it was informally called. The day consisted of formal papers, reminiscences, toasts, and letters—some delivered in person, others read by a third party. Not simply a collective appreciation and certainly not a final "thanks and good-bye," this forum was designed to engage Walter's work and person, and to describe and codify his many achievements and contributions. Beyond that, the planners, moderators, and presenters hoped to suggest and promote and prod further possibilities for Wink's work—whether by Walter himself, or by the individuals and communities which have been, and are yet to be, influenced by his work.

The volume you hold in your hand is, in large measure, a collection of what was offered at this celebration of Wink and his work, with some significant additions. Lee Hancock, then Dean of Auburn Seminary, did the complicated work of delineating the arenas and aspects of Walter's work to be addressed and identifying esteemed colleagues to offer reflections on these.

Many of these colleagues are familiar and influential within their fields; some are familiar and influential (like Wink) far beyond their particular fields; and others are less widely known, but nonetheless effective in what they do and how they do it. Those readers who are intimately knowledgeable of Wink's work, its breadth and depth, may feel confident in locating a lacuna or two. Most who are familiar with the Wink corpus (in print and in the body of workshops presented alone

8. Wink, *The Powers that Be*, 110.

and in collaboration with June Keener Wink), and certainly those newer to it, will find here, in a template and through a roster compiled largely by Hancock, a worthy and challenging reflection on, and engagement with, Wink's work.

The first section, "Powers of the Scholar," surveys the fields and disciplines with which, and within which, Wink has carried out his work. To suggest that Wink has been influential in various fields and in many ways is to state the obvious. These essays serve in large measure to recall, describe, and codify the influence that Wink has had and the importance that his work continues to have.

In his "Overview of the Work of Walter Wink: 1968 to the Present," theologian and biblical scholar Wayne Rollins proposes a framework for organizing and plotting the development of Wink's work across three major phases: Advancing the Paradigm (1973); Amplifying the Paradigm (1973–2002); and Actualizing the Paradigm (2002 to the present). The "Paradigm" of which Rollins speaks is traceable, of course, to Wink's groundbreaking *The Bible in Human Transformation*, published in 1973. Rollins helpfully identifies the seeds of Wink's later thinking that are already evident in this early work. By acknowledging and, to some degree, fleshing out, these influences and paradigms—such as Wink's reaction against the then-standard scholarly impulse to demystify the text, and the engagement of Jungian and other psychological approaches—Rollins is able to trace a helpful, if not necessarily straight, line from Wink's early and influential book on biblical studies to his more recent book, *The Human Being*.

In describing Wink's approach to historical criticism in this latter work, Rollins introduces, suggestively, a particular theme which will recur within these pages just as it recurs in Wink's work: "Wink tells us that truth is to be valued above historical accuracy," writes Rollins. What is "truth"? And for that matter, what is "historical accuracy"? Rollins deftly pursues Wink's claim that all quests for the historical Jesus are "mythic" in content and agenda. Finally, he includes a "wish" list of issues for Wink to pursue—and, I might add, for those influenced by Wink's work to pursue, as well. That there is much still to be actualized on all of the major fronts opened up by Wink's work is no slight to Wink and his efforts. Quite the opposite: from this fertile practitioner, there is much yet to be harvested.

Bruce Chilton, a biblical scholar and, like Wink, an original member of the Jesus Seminar, considers "Walter Wink and Biblical Scholarship." Although he begins with Walter's first, and important, publication, *John the Baptist and the Gospel Tradition* (1968), and personal memories of Wink's participation, as a young professor, in a seminar on biblical criticism, Chilton does not mean to write chronologically or extensively about Wink's output *per se*. Rather, he turns to suggestive and qualitative considerations of Walter's work as a whole, noting, for example, that admissions of "discontent and even . . . frustration" are leitmotifs of Walter's work and among the many reasons he is considered a seminal scholar. Through both action and reaction, and sometimes a complicated combination of the two, Wink's work begins to take shape within the field of biblical studies and, by (seemingly organic) extension, beyond.

J. Harold Ellens, who convened a scholarly panel on Wink's *The Human Being* at the annual meeting of the Society of Biblical Literature in November 2002, considers "Walter Wink and Hermeneutics" broadly through the "impressive spate of sturdy books" that anchors the Wink corpus, and specifically through a pointed and helpful summary of *The Human Being*. His findings are relevant not only for that recent volume, but suggest approaches for thinking about Wink's work as a whole.

New Testament scholar and former Wink student Sharon H. Ringe shifts the primary focus from the printed page to the embodied, present teacher as she reflects on "Walter Wink and Pedagogy." Wink's methods and practice as a teacher, she says, helped her to experience "a relationship to the [scriptural] text that I would call 'iconic.'" Tellingly, she adds later in the essay, that it was "both *what* he taught me, and *how* he taught me" that have shaped her work as a teacher and scholar.

With the essay by philosopher and independent scholar D. Seiple, "Walter Wink and Philosophy," there is another shift, this one to disciplines besides biblical studies, to other arenas with and within which Wink works. In a statement both personal and professional, Seiple posits that Wink's is "a thoroughly philosophical project," perhaps even, in some of its specifics, a project that points to the "most profound" philosophical issues and questions of our time. Too, this essay revisits that knotty problem raised by Rollins—the vexing issue of "historical accuracy" versus "truth."

Ted Grimsrud, theologian and expert in Peace Studies, takes up the matter of "Walter Wink and Peace Theology." Put simply, Grimsrud argues that "Walter has helped unlock a world of resources from the biblical tradition that are needed in our world today." Grimsrud highlights some of these resources, along with their (potential) applications, while also digging deeper for something of the essence, and hope, of Wink's work.

As if reflecting and building on Seiple's approach, Hal Childs, who directs the California Counseling Institute, makes the matter of "Walter Wink and Psychology" both professional and personal, even to the point of personalizing Psyche. How has engagement with psychology influenced Wink's work and the field of biblical studies more broadly? How too, in Childs' words, has Wink "changed psychology"? The answers, and even soundings in the direction of answers, aren't easy, and they elicit, in Childs' treatment, somewhat violent words and images—"collision," "wrestling." At the same time, they provide insights into, and open new possibilities for, Wink's work.

The second section of the book provides a unique window onto Wink's legacy and a particular opportunity for engaging it. Though less systematic than the essays in the first section, the "Testimonials and Toasts" in Section Two extend the reflections of those essays. Here you'll find colleagues, collaborators, and former students reflecting on Wink's work and his contributions to their own work. In their informality and differences of style and tone, these contributions suggest something of the flavor and interplay that marked Walter's retirement celebration. In so doing, they offer a glimpse of what it has been like to be shaped by Walter's *presence* and *teaching*, and the interpretive and facilitating work that he and June undertake together.

To draw on a word used by Robert Raines, a sometime Wink collaborator, these reminiscences, summations, praises, and parting shots witness to one whose work itself stands as witness. And so, within his "Toast," activist Richard Deats recalls not only the publication of *Jesus' Third Way*, but the very real-life drama behind its distribution in South Africa as the Apartheid era was drawing to a close—including the challenges of smuggling its author into the country to address grass-roots groups.

A couple of fellow New Testament scholars, Marcus Borg and Amy-Jill Levine, each share something of their engagements and histories with Wink and his work. Borg's helpful summations augment statements by Rollins and others in Section One, while Levine's correctives—"To sum up Walter's contributions is impossible," and, "I don't think there should be a summation yet"—are themselves difficult to dispute. I'd suggest letting these different approaches stand as further (unresolved) tensions vis-à-vis the Wink corpus.

Robert Evans, founder and director of the Plowshares Institute, organizes a good bit of his commentary around the Winkian concept of "Transformation," while Tansy Chapman, Episcopal priest and retreat leader, focuses on two notions more directly associated with June Keener Wink, "Integration and Embodiment." Picking up on threads which run through both of these statements, Bonnie Rosborough, a former Wink student and congregational minister, writes of Walter's modeling of "God's gifts," and the opportunities and challenges they bespeak, which are both "precious and demanding."

Of the contributions which round out the section, that of the late Rabbi Balfour Brickner poignantly moves from humor, through a concise summary of Wink's work on homosexuality and the Bible, to personal reflection on the real people affected by—and not simply the concepts and constructs that inform—debates and decisions about homosexuality within religious communities: "As a Jew, I know well . . . what cruelty such thinking can unleash. I have been its victim. We all have." Consistent with Wink's option for hope, Barbara Wheeler, President of Auburn Seminary, asserts that Wink's work has "convinced many people, outside the church as well as in it, that the Bible is a means of power, the power with which God graces all of us to love and heal the world." In his toast, Raines draws on Wink's statement, quoted earlier in Ringe's essay, that "history belongs to the intercessors who believe the future into being."

What that future might entail, at least in terms of continued challenges to and from Wink's work, is the stuff of the final section, "Enigmas of the Future." Taking a cue, perhaps, from Wink himself, the contributors here don't simply rest easy with Wink's work. They are themselves moved by, and see important potentialities for, continued engagement.

Joseph C. Hough, president of Union Theological Seminary in New York City, was invited to contribute to this volume and responded with "A New Spirituality and Hope for the Future: Some Contributions from the Scholarship of Walter Wink." Like Grimsrud, Hough sees an urgency in applying the insights of Wink's work not only within the academy, but to the world more broadly. In particular, and in some detail, Hough considers a Winkian response to the "apocalyptic frenzy" that he finds within American religious and political thought today. Further, he finds in Wink's work "new possibilities" for Christian mysticism and Christian openness to the spiritual insights of other religious traditions.

Well-known author Jack Miles was also asked to contribute to this volume. In response, he took on the scholarly and practical problem of "The Christ of Mere Literature." To some degree, his essay continues the discussion, referenced in Ellens' essay and elsewhere in this volume, of a recurring tension within Wink's work: that of the "historical" or "historiographical" versus a number of other concepts, approaches, and terms including "artful composite" (Miles' term) or "myth" (more familiar within Wink's writings). Picking up the threads of an earlier scholarly exchange in the journal *CrossCurrents*,[9] Miles promotes "the opposition between historical and aesthetic modes of appropriation," and thus begins to construct his own defensible and practical (though perhaps as yet unfinished) framework, while at the same challenging and appropriating what he finds most useful and provocative in Wink's work.

Author, activist, and teacher Alastair McIntosh rounds out this short list (Hough, Miles, and McIntosh) of those whose contributions post-date the May 2005 event. His essay, "Engaging Walter Wink's Powers—an Activist's Testimony," formulates, describes, and invites what he refers to as "the imperative of involvement." Through theological reflection, direct engagement of several of Wink's work (including *Engaging the Powers*, "the most important activist's handbook that I have ever encountered), and intellectual and activist autobiography, McIntosh tells a story—several stories, really—about how one (along with many others!) can, and has, put "hands" on that which he has learned from Wink, adopting and adapting Wink's work directly in such areas as land reform in his native Scotland, corporate engagement of—and for—the environment, and training in on-violence for military leaders.

9. *Cross Currents*, Summer 2003; see esp. Wink, "Response to Jack Miles."

In "From the Past to the Future of Biblical Activism," activist and pastor Bill Wylie-Kellerman plots the influence of Wink's work as it has moved from the academy out into other arenas and recalls Wink's specific work in more activist venues—such as the features he co-edited for *Fellowship*. Though *The Human Being* "resumes the direct conversation with the biblical guild," Wylie-Kellermann outlines particular ways that it, and Wink's work more generally, continues to influence individuals and communities engaged in activism.

In his essay, "What's Next?," theologian and ethicist Ray Gingerich draws on the biblical imagery of "surrounding" and "redeeming" Jericho. Though Gingerich himself questions how far he might, or should, push the image, it nevertheless serves as a reminder of the depth of Wink's analyses as applied both to the biblical text and to the work of individuals and communities.

Richard Deats' final prayer calls on the "gracious" God, who is the source of "hope," to "help us to give ourselves anew to engaging the powers and to do so with determination, faith, and compassion." As I write this Introduction, on that day set aside in the liturgical calendar for remembering "The Holy Innocents" of Matthew 2:16–18, I cannot but recall Wink's moving discussions of the innocents "disappeared" from *barrios* and *favelas*,[10] and of the various systems of domination around the world which are engaging, even now, in such behavior. I hope that this volume will serve as a call and a challenge to maintain and build on the breadth of Walter Wink's work—from the academic to the ecclesiastical to the political, from the theoretical to the practical. May it inspire in its readers both the will and the means to search for the truth, and to "frustrate the designs of evil tyrants and establish [God's] rule of justice, love, and peace."[11]

---

10. Wink, *Naming the Powers*, ix.

11. The Prayer of the Day, The Holy Innocents, Martyrs, *The Lutheran Book of Worship*, 31.

Powers *of the* Scholar

1

An Overview of the Work of Walter Wink

1968 to the Present

Wayne G. Rollins

WALTER WINK'S PUBLISHED WORK BEGINS KNEE-DEEP IN THE HEAD-waters of the Jordan River with John the Baptist—in more ways than one. When the publication of his *John the Baptist and the Gospel Tradition* was warmly welcomed by the guild of biblical scholars in 1968, no one would have guessed how prophetic the relationship between Walter and the man of locusts and wild honey would be. Only a few years later, Walter found himself assuming the role of *vox clamantis in deserto* with the publication of his second book, *The Bible in Human Transformation*, and its opening proclamation that "historical biblical criticism is bankrupt."[1] Everything to date in Walter's professional life and work follows from that moment.

Walter did his best to explain that by "bankrupt" he did not mean to imply something "valueless, or useless." Historical biblical criticism is "bankrupt," he maintained, "solely because it is incapable of achieving what most of its practitioners considered its purpose to be: so to interpret the Scriptures that the past becomes alive and illumines our present with new possibilities for personal and social transformation."[2] Some biblical scholars heard his message; others did not. Walter's detractors were many and even his employers failed to appreciate the point. Three decades later, however, it has become clear how his voice has informed a

1. Wink, *The Bible in Human Transformation*, 1.
2. Ibid., 1–2.

3

body of opinion which acknowledges this very point—that biblical texts have to do not only with the past, but with perennial personal and social transformation, even for scholars.

But as important as Walter's first sentence was, it is the book's subtitle that touches on the longer view and the larger battle plan. It reads: "Toward a New Paradigm for Biblical Study." The word "paradigm" appears in each chapter heading of the book. How this paradigm looked in 1973 and how it is evolving in 2005 constitute the subject of this paper, in three parts: Part One: Advancing the Paradigm (1973); Part Two: Amplifying the Paradigm (1973–2002); Part Three: Actualizing the Paradigm (2002 to the present).

Part One: Advancing the Paradigm (1973)

In 1973, Wink's manifesto volume on *The Bible in Human Transformation* performed a *critical* and *constructive* task within the world of biblical scholarship.

The *critical task* was captured in the words of Luke 11:52, a virtual legend over the doorway of Wink's work: "Woe to you Scholars! For you have taken away the key of knowledge; you did not enter yourselves, and you hindered those who were entering."[3] Wink's book rehearsed the critiques of historical biblical scholarship, and he was not completely alone in this. He cited as allies James Smart, Amos Wilder, Bob Funk, James Robinson, and Bard Childs. The check-list of critiques is now familiar: the "ideology of objectivism"; the "fiction of detachment"; the imposition of a subject-object dichotomy that reduces the text to a passive object under the scrutiny of an all-seeing scholar's eye; a technologism that regards as legitimate only those questions its own methods are designed to answer.[4] But for Wink, perhaps the most serious charge was the "demystification of the text" and the loss of the "numinous"—a criticism that reflected Carl Jung's critique of biblical criticism in his Terry lectures at Yale forty years earlier:

> Nor has scientific criticism . . . been very helpful in enhancing belief in the . . . scriptures. It is . . . a fact that under the influence of a so-called scientific enlightenment great masses of educated people have either left the church or have become pro-

3. Ibid., 81.
4. Ibid., 7–8.

foundly indifferent to it. If they were all dull rationalists or neurotic intellectuals, the loss would not be regrettable. But many of them are religious people . . . .[5]

The book's *constructive* task was to call for a new paradigm, citing the thesis in T. S. Kuhn's widely read *The Structure of Scientific Revolution* that even in science, new paradigms are necessary to correct the occupational blindness of the old.[6] Though Wink's new paradigm was *in nuce* in 1973, it advanced three hermeneutical approaches that would characterize Wink's future work and leave a permanent mark on the guild: (1) autobiographical hermeneutics, (2) psychological hermeneutics, and (3) "communal hermeneutics."

Autobiographical hermeneutics. Before it was fashionable, Wink realized the importance of autobiographical "confession" for scholars. In his 1973 book, he introduced himself as "a white male in a liberal Protestant Seminary." And he added a telling interpretive footnote: "I have gone my own way."[7] More than any biblical scholar I know, Wink has made explicit what is often unacknowledged—that all scholarship is autobiographical. Wink makes this clear in everything he writes, alluding to his experiences in Chile, South and Central America, and South Africa, his experience with a group of Sunday school teen-agers in Manhattan, and in a Texas parish. Wink's fundamental hermeneutical objective is to engage the deep questions addressed in the pages of Scripture with the deep questions of life lived in all of these places.

Wink cites Jürgen Habermas' *Knowledge and Human Interests* and its thesis that "*interest* precedes knowledge." This stands in stark contrast to the "objectivist's concept of knowledge as pure theory untouched by the practical concerns of life." Habermas insists that in all scholarship, "*interest* is not an interest in knowledge for knowledge's sake but an interest in knowledge as enlightenment . . . ."[8]

What is the interest at work in Wink's biblical scholarship? His answer: to learn more about "that something" that "speaks through the text [and] which called the text and myself into being."[9] For Wink, we

5. Jung, *The Collected Works*, 11:34.
6. Kuhn, *The Structure of Scientific Revolutions.*
7. Wink, *The Bible in Human Transformation*, iii.
8. Ibid., 69–70.
9. Ibid., 74.

are not in this business for nothing, certainly not just for publication; we're in it for "life."

Psychological hermeneutics. A second bold stroke in Wink's 1973 book, beyond the declaration of bankruptcy, was his allusion to "The Guild for Psychological Studies in San Francisco." As late as the 1970s, a reference to psychology in biblical critical circles was enough to raise eyebrows, if not cook one's professional goose. Though not fully developed, Wink's psychological hermeneutic is informed on the one hand by (a) Freud, Gadamer, Ricoeur, and David Bakan; and on the other by (b) Jung and Erich Neumann.

(a) The Freudian element is expressed in Wink's goal to "liberate the symbolic function" of the Bible, based on the premise that symbols give rise not only to thought but to the "becoming" of the reader. Thus the goal of research is not only the "archaeology of the object" (the text) but, to use the well-worn Riceoeurian phrase, the "archaeology of the subject" (the scholar/reader).

(b) The Jungian contribution is twofold. On the one hand it provides insight into the archetypal power of biblical imagery. A passage I have cited many times, to illustrate the nature of archetypes, comes from Wink's 1978 article, "On Wrestling with God: Using Psychological Insights in Biblical Study." He writes:

> This motif of wrestling with a spirit to obtain a blessing appears so frequently in widely scattered mythic traditions that we are justified in regarding [them] . . . as a standard component in spiritual development. The very pervasiveness of such stories . . . is evidence that we are dealing with something fundamental to the spiritual journey itself, and not merely with etiological legends invented to "explain the origin of things.[10]

A second "Jungian" contribution comes from the pedagogical paradigm developed by Dr. Elizabeth Howes of the Guild for Psychological Studies. The method demonstrates in a group context how texts can precipitate an "archaeology of the subject." By 1983, Wink had developed his own three-stage version of the method, published in his widely disseminated book, *Transforming Bible Study*. Wink and his wife June also demonstrated this method on site in hundreds of Bible study workshops in the United States and abroad. Wink calls it a "dialectical hermeneutic."

10. Wink, "On Wrestling with God," 142.

He tells us, "The insights we seek by means of the text are . . . neither general religious or theological truths, nor simply the author's original insights, but the truth of our own personal and social being as it is laid bare by dialectical interpretation of the text."[11]

Communal hermeneutics. A word should be said about a feature of Wink's work perhaps less visible than the others, namely "communal exegesis" or "communion" in hermeneutics, a theme resonating throughout his work. Wink wrote in 1973:

> Biblical scholars must resist the temptation of establishing themselves as scribal mandarins jealously pocketing the keys of knowledge. And the oppressed and non-expert must avoid the temptation of anti-intellectualism, and that form of "pneumatic exegesis" which simply reads off the text what one already thinks he knows. How much each could learn from the other, if only they could more often be seated around the same table![12]

Wink proposes what might be called a "Yeshiva" model of biblical study, one in which "collegiality" engages in barrages of exchange around the text, with much sound, much feverish debate, and on occasion, awe. It envisions communion between reader and text, both serving alternately as subject and object. It envisions a communion of the text's "horizons" merging with the horizon of the reader (à la Gadamer). It envisions communion between reader and reader to hear what each has heard. It envisions communion of the reader's life-questions with the life-questions that gave birth to the texts.

In metaphysical tones, Wink asks, "What is the objective of communal exegesis?" The answer: "Not the quest for certainty about things known, but the search for the unknown."[13]

Part Two: Amplifying the Paradigm (1973 to 2002)

In the twenty-nine year stretch from 1973–2002, Wink has dedicated himself to four major enterprises: a descent into and an analysis of the principalities and powers; reflection on non-violent responses to structures of domination; the development of "transforming Bible study," to which we have just alluded; and the Jesus Seminar.

11. Wink, *Transforming Bible Study*, 64.

12. Wink, *The Bible and Human Transformation*, 77.

13. Ibid., 78.

One finds a fascinating note of things to come in Wink's 1973 *The Bible in Human Transformation*: "We are dealing with not simply false notions but an alienating ethos: *a principality and power* which shapes not only our thoughts, but our life-styles, self-images, ambitions, commitments and values" (italics added).[14] In an autobiographical essay published in 1994, Wink tells us how his preoccupation with the "powers" grew:

> On the scholarly front, William Stringfellow's *Free in Obedience* (New York: Seabury, 1964) had provided me a vision of how the biblical category of principalities and powers could serve as the basis for a social ethic based on the New Testament. The received wisdom till then was that the New Testament is only concerned with personal ethics; if one is interested in a social ethic, one must turn to the Exodus or the prophets. Work on the Powers series, first conceived as a single volume, grew into three, and occupied 28 years. The titles in the Powers trilogy are: *Naming the Powers: The Language of Power in the New Testament* (1984); *Unmasking the Powers: The Invisible Forces that Determine Human Existence* (1986); and *Engaging the Powers: Discernment and Resistance in a World of Domination* (1992). A related volume, *Cracking the Gnostic Code*, rounds out the understanding of the Powers in the early centuries of our era.[15]

Out of a desire to better understand the dark side of "the Powers," Wink traveled with his wife, June, on a sabbatical leave to Chile in 1982, to experience first hand the military dictatorship of General Augusto Pinochet in Chile. He visited other parts of South and Central America as well, to see the barrios, the notorious *favelas*, and to speak with nuns and priests who were working for human rights and with defense lawyers searching for the "disappeared ones." These experiences led to reflection on strategies for combating oppressive systems of domination and on the soul-troubling question of a non-violent stance.

> I became increasingly convinced that nonviolence was the only way to overcome the domination of the Powers without creating new forms of domination. I decided to test this hunch in South Africa, where we spent part of a sabbatical in 1986. On our return I wrote a little book, *Violence and Nonviolence in South Africa* (Philadelphia: New Society Publishers, 1987) which

14. Wink, *Transforming Bible Study*, 82.

15. Wink, "Write What You See," n.p.

urged the churches of South Africa to become more involved in nonviolent direct action against the apartheid regime.[16]

This book was later published in a modestly bound South African version, under the title *Jesus' Third Way.*

What is the "third way"? It is a third option to two standard approaches to violence. The first of these standard approaches is the acceptance of violence as the only means to secure the peace—an attitude Wink describes brilliantly as grounded in a "Myth of Redemptive Violence").[17] The second is a nonviolent route that is passive and refuses to coerce or resist in any form. The "third way" of Jesus, as Wink discerns it, is another genre, a *resistant* nonviolence, one that is confrontational and coercive, without being lethal. It is the nonviolence of Gandhi, Dorothy Day, Leo Tolstoy, Martin Luther King Jr, and César Chavez. It is the resistant nonviolence that Witness for Peace initiated in the warring environments of Nicaragua, El Salvador, Guatemala and Haiti. It is the resistant nonviolence forged by the collaboration of Catholics and Protestants that challenged the Marcos dictatorship in the Philippines, that brought an end to the genocide inaugurated by the Soviets in Lithuania, that resisted the Nazi pogroms in Finland, Norway, Denmark, Holland, and Bulgaria. It is the resistant nonviolence that is imagined in the enjoiners to turn the other cheek and walk the extra mile, designed to confront and raise the consciousness of the oppressor. It is the resistant nonviolence that insists on the impossible assignment of loving one's enemies, which Wink describes as "a way of living in expectation of miracles."[18]

In 1994, Wink wrote of his inclination and decision to move beyond the Jesus Seminar with which he had been fruitfully engaged. He writes:

> My greatest hesitation about the Jesus Seminar is the idea that it is possible to build, from the bottom up, a perspective-free, objective database. Such a neutral, "pictureless" standpoint is impossible. Every analysis is value-laden. We cannot help projecting onto the texts our own unconscious needs and desires for transformation or confirmation, to say nothing of our socio-political location and biases. We need to take seriously the

16. Ibid., n.p.

17. Wink, *The Powers That Be*, 56–62.

18. Ibid., 178.

implications of the Heisenberg principle: that the observer is always a part of the field being observed, and disturbs that field by the very act of observation . . .

Thus liberals will tend to construct a liberal Jesus, conservatives a conservative Jesus, pietists a pietistic Jesus, radicals a radical Jesus, and atheists an unattractive Jesus. Scholars who believe Jesus was like a cynic philosopher will tend to reject as non-historical any data that suggests otherwise. When the cynic school prevailed, for example, in the voting at the Jesus Seminar, the apocalypticists quit coming; this further skewed the vote. The Seminar is denied the fresh perspective that liberationists and feminists might bring since there are almost no women or non-Caucasians in the group. So the picture that is emerging of Jesus is remarkably like that of a tweedy professor interested in studying Scripture.

I have abandoned the quest for the historical Jesus, conceived as an objective, value-free endeavor. Instead, I am in quest of the originative impulse released by Jesus, and will value traditions regardless of their source, so long as they are faithful to that originative impulse. So I intend to ignore the Seminar's database and voting tabulations when I begin to write on the Son of Man.[19]

Wink achieved this objective with the 2002 publication of *The Human Being: Jesus and the Enigma of the Son of the Man*—manifesting the paradigm that had been manifesto in 1973.

Part Three: Actualizing the Paradigm: "The Human Being" (2002)

In 2002, Wink published *The Human Being: Jesus and The Enigma of the Son of the Man,* a *tour de force* of historical, literary, and psychological insight that fulfilled the paradigmatic aspirations voiced in *The Bible and Human Transformation* in 1973. I would like to say a few words of appreciation for the book's scholarly virtuosity and then comment on two aspects of the book that epitomize its paradigmatic achievement within the field of biblical scholarship.

The Human Being is a virtuoso combination of historical and literary criticism, of ethics, philosophy (Ludwig Feuerbach has an entire chapter), spirituality, etymology, *Geistesgeschichte* (which means not

19 Wink, "Write What You See."

only the history of ideas but also of the strong cross-cultural currents that move in the human psyche), depth psychology, and even a touch of neurophysiology.

The biblical scholar will find here a feast of original exegetical insight in well-traveled Synoptic territory, but also, virtually for the first time, the full inclusion of the Fourth Gospel as a worthy interlocutor in conversation about the impulse that the historical Jesus inaugurated in the human psyche. Above all, the book alters forever the way in which the Son-of-the-Man passages will be read by all of us who have read Wink's book. It achieves this by placing the discussion in a totally new context, namely, the process whereby the Son-of-the-Man image emerges as a heuristic force within the human psyche.

Two features of the book that warrant special attention with respect to Wink's 1973 paradigm are his stance on classical historical biblical criticism and his stance on psychological-critical insight as a required piece of equipment for the complete historian.

Wink's stance on classical historical biblical criticism. Although the main body of Wink's book is a monument to the best of classical historical scholarship, Wink makes it clear that "getting the historical facts right" is not the endgame. Three examples indicate Wink's considerable remove from the older orthodoxies of the historical-critical method and, by implication, from the Jesus seminar.

First he spells out his method, telling us he will "not seek to get *behind* the text" as much as to "penetrate deeply *into* the texts." "I employ historical-critical tools wherever they seem appropriate," Wink tells us. But he also wants us to see the text as "the Sinai of the Soul, where God still speaks," hardly a run-of-the-mill historical-critical objective.[20]

Second, with respect to the objectives of critical scholarship, Wink tells us that truth is to be valued above historical accuracy. Wink intriguingly insists that his goal is to determine not so much "whether Jesus actually said something, but whether it is true, regardless of who said it."[21] To illustrate his point he adds a flourish seldom heard on the plains of historical biblical scholarship, quoting Black Elk, the Lakota Sioux:

20. Wink, *The Human Being*, 5.
21. Ibid.,15.

"This they tell, and whether it happened so or not I do not know but if you think about it, you can see that it is true."[22]

Third, concurring with the thesis of *The Myth of History and the Evolution of Consciousness,* an important volume authored by his former student Hal Childs, Wink declares that all attempts to reclaim the historical Jesus are mythic in content and agenda, and that the goal of historical Jesus research from the perspective of psychological realism (in Childs' words) is to contribute to "the evolution of consciousness, both for the individual and for culture . . . in the service of self-understanding and world-understanding."[23] Or in Wink's words: "True, the quest for the historical Jesus has not presented Jesus 'as he really was.' Rather, that quest has all along been the largely unconscious search for a Jesus who can bring us to life."[24]

Wink on psychological-critical insight. One of the lasting contributions of Wink's work is his insistence on approaching his subject with what Hal Childs has called "psychological realism." *Historical* realism tells us about physical, economic, social, and political facts and factors on the human scene; *psychological* realism tells us about the psychic facts and factors in the human scene. These psychic facts and factors are cut from both conscious and unconscious cloth, and they permeate all human activity. They are "real" and have "real effects." They operate in the individual and in the collective. And they are at work at the heart of Jesus research, both in its method and motive, as much as they are in my speaking this sentence and your listening. They may in the end prove to be the most decisive determinants of what a text includes, why its sayings and stories were remembered, for what purpose it is written, how it is read, and how it affects both human lives and human history.

I would like to offer two examples of psychic factors Wink would have us consider. The first is Wink's portrait of the collective unconscious at work in the promulgation of the Son of the Man archetype—the major thesis of the book. Wink invites us to observe "around the beginning of the first millennium, the explosion of a massive archetypal mutation: an inner Anthropos, a divine child, born of the divine Human—a hom-

22. Ibid., 112.

23. Childs, *The Myth of the Historical Jesus and the Evolution of Consciousness,* 260.

24. Wink, *Human Being,* 112.

ing device orienting us toward our true selves."[25] This revelation "had steadily been asserting itself from the time of Ezekiel forward, and was now affecting everything in its path. It not only dominated Christian and Jewish theology and mystical practice, but manifested itself in a novel way in Gnosticism, and within the bosom of Islam, in Sufism."[26]

A second example is a phenomenon that Wink mentions on the first page of the book: "the original *impulse* of Jesus" (italics added). "My goal," Wink states, "is to recover what Jesus unleashed—the original impulse that prompted the spread of his message."[27] Wink is probing the alchemy that occurs between the historic Jesus and those individuals whose psyche, conscience, will, and vision have been catalyzed by the encounter. Wink quotes an oft-cited psychological insight of Carl Jung that *the impulse* is as much a function of the hearer as it is of the historical Jesus who unleashed it:

> Christ would never have made the impression he did on his followers if he had not expressed something that was alive and at work in their unconscious. Christianity itself would never have spread through the pagan world with such astonishing rapidity had its ideas not found an analogous psychic readiness to receive them.[28]

This is but a sampling of a vastly complex book that takes giant steps through centuries of religious traditions and invites reading and rereading for the treasures it holds and for the healthy debates that it inspires.

Wink has told us something of his future plans beyond *The Human Being*. "In a sequel, I will search for clues about *how* to be more human."[29] Wink's own polymorphous virtuosity has already demonstrated his humanity in the past thirty-two years. But beyond that, I would wish for a primer for readers of *The Human Being* who need a refresher course on archetypal psychology, so that they might catch the full drift of the psychological substratum in his work—perhaps an *Archetypes for Dummies*. I also hope that he will extend his exploration of the archetypal

25. Ibid., 247.
26. Ibid., 229.
27. Ibid., 13.
28. Ibid., 151.
29. Ibid., xi.

power of the Son-of-the-Man mythos by probing what lies anchored deep within the broad range of Christian traditions—its creeds and dogmas, its litanies and ecclesiastical utterances, its magisterial teaching and its monastic discipline. This would help us develop sensitivity for the myriad configurations the tradition has developed for voicing and incarnating the archetype of human and divine wholeness.

Beyond this and above all, Wink's work to date is an extraordinary achievement for the historical development of biblical scholarship and its public appreciation. He has provided a paradigm for bringing together two sets of worlds formerly quarantines from one another. More than any other biblical scholar I know, Walter has bridged the gap between scholarship and life, between systems of domination and cells of nonviolent resistance, between the lucid rationality of consciousness and the numinous dreams, myths, and archetypal images of the unconscious, between the rationally objective and passionately subjective, between body and psyche, between book and being. And at the heart of it all, he honors the continuum he expresses in the opening paragraph *The Powers That Be*. There, Walter Wink writes:

> This book is unashamedly about things spiritual. It assumes that spiritual reality is at the heart of everything, from photons to supernovas, from a Little League baseball team to Boeing Aircraft. It sees spirit as the capacity to be aware of and responsive to God—at the core of every institution, every city, every nation, every corporation, every place of worship . . . . What I have written celebrates a divine reality that pervades every aspect of our existence, where the harmony intended for the universe can already begin to be experienced. And it invites those who are suffering from spiritual malnutrition to a heavenly feast like nothing this society can offer.[30]

30. Wink, *The Powers That Be*, 13.

2

Walter Wink and Biblical Scholarship

Bruce Chilton

I AM GRATEFUL TO WALTER WINK AND LEE HANCOCK FOR LETTING me join in this wonderful occasion, as it were, from outside the family. You have given me the opportunity to review not only a corpus of work, but also a collegial contact over a number of years. Much of the value of Walter's contribution to the discipline of New Testament study eluded me until I reflected back on his persona as well as on his writing.

∽

I first met Walter, not in person but in print, by means of his book *John the Baptist and the Gospel Tradition*. Why exactly I picked it up, I could not tell you now anymore than I could have told you at the time (in 1972). The book wasn't assigned in any Master of Divinity class in my seminary; I was no doubt skipping some assignment in order to leaf through its pages. Since I found the volume in St. Mark's Library at the General Theological Seminary, I should have regarded the author with some suspicion, as among the Protestant reductionists uptown. But instead I stopped leafing through *John the Baptist and the Gospel Tradition*, started reading properly in a chair with a straight back, and finished the book in a sitting. It offered an extraordinarily clean approach to the major methods of biblical criticism that were used at the time, focused on a fundamental question of history and exegesis.

But then, the wonder of the book is that it has the courage to end on a note of dissatisfaction. The willingness to admit discontent and even to emphasize frustration is a leitmotif in Walter's work, one of the things that makes him a seminal scholar. In *John the Baptist,* he is dissatisfied that, having applied the objectifying methods of conventional biblical study, he winds up with objective data, rather than a pattern of meaning with which a person can engage.

This dissatisfaction is not the usual, pro-forma complaint about the paucity of data I frequently hear from colleagues. In the field of New Testament study, scholars waste perfectly good ink on the page and oxygen during conferences whining that they haven't enough "facts" to work with. I wish I had a nickel for every hand-wringing exegete who has said, "If only we had more data about Jesus." But the complainants are the same scholars who *ignore* ninety percent of the Gospels, on the grounds that they are not "objective." The thought of moving by more informed inference (rather than deduction) from the Gospels to the events that generated them does not cross their minds, because objectivism prohibits that move. Walter's complaint is different and more profound.

Instead, Walter has observed that history, rather than being a collection of supposedly objective data, is really a pattern of human meaning. You might embrace that pattern or reject it, but any history that does not address us at the level of pattern and meaning is not worthy of the name. To complain about one's own results, especially in a dissertation that later appeared as a book with the Cambridge University Press, does not represent a run-of-the-mill approach to building a career. Walter's idea of history, grounded in philosophical and historiographic discussion, directly contradicted the positivistic fashions of New Testament work current at the time.

Two years after I read *John the Baptist,* the late Father Raymond Brown invited me up to the seminar he conducted here at the Union Theological Seminary. (He was kind enough to allow me in, although I was not yet a doctoral student, at the suggestion of Professor Schuyler Brown at General.) Ray convened that seminar in order to begin systematic work on the Passion narratives, and his project ultimately became the book *The Death of the Messiah.*[1] Early on in those proceedings Walter attended, not as a student (as I was), but as a grown-up professor.

That was my first personal meeting with Walter. He will not recollect the event, although we have both enjoyed conversations at

---

1. Brown, *Death of the Messiah.*

subsequent meetings. But that first time I was concealed under an inordinate amount of hair (and under the cloud of coming from the wrong seminary). From the natural cave in which I dwelled, I could look out at speakers and study some of their expressions as well as their hearers' reactions. The tension between Ray Brown and Walter Wink was sometimes unspoken, sometimes articulate, but always palpable. Walter could not have been much concerned with new interlopers; he had the biggest of fish to fry.

Ray Brown defended his objectifying view of history and of the exegete's task with great passion. Walter Wink asserted the contrary, engaged view of history without having to search for his words, because at that stage his book, *The Bible in Human Transformation: Toward a New Paradigm for Biblical Study*, had just come out. I can't remember his precise expressions, but Walter might well have said, in the early days of that seminar, what he writes at the beginning of his book *The Human Being*:

> What stands in the way of new/ancient readings of Scripture is the heritage of positivism and objectivism—the belief that we can handle these radioactive texts without ourselves being irradiated. Biblical scholars have been exceedingly slow to grasp the implications of the Heisenberg Principle: that the observer is always part of the field being observed and disturbs that field by the very act of observation.[2]

At the time I was astounded both by the insight and the simplicity of the statement that Walter had made, breaching the largely unreflective[3] fashion among New Testament scholars, who assumed that they could pursue history entirely on the basis of the collection of data even as the understanding of history elsewhere, in fields cognate with theirs, was changing radically.

How and *why* it was changing, I think, I must leave to other speakers, because I want to move on to the way in which Walter, once he posed this challenge in his mind, then began to devise responses to that

2. Wink, *The Human Being*, 7.

3. I say "largely unreflective" to allow room for the tactical stance of Ray Brown himself, who defended his positivistic perspective to some extent as a counterweight to what he saw as the increasing dogmatism of the Vatican. There is some irony here, because Walter's position involves a correction of the "historically" grounded dogmas of Protestant theology.

challenge. He did so in his book *Naming the Powers*, in which he further articulates his deep dissatisfaction with what he calls reductionism in the historical critical study of the Bible. Not content with that, he also criticizes liberation theologians for their similar tendencies. "Reductionist explanations," he writes, "are inadequate because they omit the one essential most unique to the New Testament understanding of power: its spiritual dimension." He goes on to say, "There is a certain irony in the fact that liberation theologians have, in the main, followed the reductionist path and treated the powers as *just* institutions and systems with little attempt to comprehend their spiritual dimension or take seriously their mythic form."[4]

That's what his whole trilogy, *The Powers*, undertakes.[5] It is a huge effort, more than a trilogy, because Walter has also written sequels, and *The Bible and Human Transformation* amounts to a prequel. Unlike George Lucas's prequel, which is being advertised this week, Walter brought his prequel, trilogy, and sequel out in real-time order, and therefore the corpus is much more consistent. I recommend reading them in order for precisely that reason. Their technology is always getting better. Unlike the special effects of *Star Wars*, they get less and less baroque, the prose more and more scarified and precise. And the insistence grows, already apparent in *Naming the Powers*, that a principle of uncertainty, such as the one Heisenberg crafted, is necessary in all historical study and in all critical grounded action.

In speaking of uncertainty, Walter rejects projection and relativism as having any part in the idiom of history. "In biblical studies," he writes, "word studies are the equivalent of field exploration in mineral classification in geology."[6] And he undertakes field exploration with exacting insistence. The primary texts are all there in the trilogy; secondary literature on the powers is engaged as well as the powers themselves. The result is that Walter brings together linguistics with lucid patterns of meaning.

In a single sentence he is able to summarize New Testament scholarship, mount a brilliant critique of a dissertation produced from

---

4. Wink, *Naming the Powers*, 103.

5. Wink's *Powers* trilogy includes *Naming the Powers; Unmasking the Powers;* and *Engaging the Powers*. After the trilogy proper, among other works see *Cracking the Gnostic Code; When the Powers Fall;* and *Jesus and Nonviolence*.

6. Wink, *Naming the Powers*, 35.

the department in which I was then working (Biblical Studies at the University of Sheffield in England), and at the same time articulate a new understanding of how we should understand the powers in New Testament mythology:

> I suggest that the "angels of nature" are the patterning of physical things—rocks, trees, plants, the whole God-glorifying, dancing, visible universe; that the "principalities and powers" are the inner or spiritual essence, or gestalt, of an institution or state or system; that the "demons" are the psychic or spiritual power emanated by organizations or individuals or subaspects of individuals whose energies are bent on overpowering others.[7]

Walter here combines an enormous amount of what other biblical scholars would call data, with an insight into the patterns of those data and how we apprehend them as cognitive human beings.

He goes on in that same sentence, as you might expect, to speak of Satan. But I think he deals with evil more fully, much better, and in a way that hones his own rhetoric as a New Testament scholar to its finest edge, in his book *Unmasking the Powers*, which appeared in 1986. He writes there, "The demonic confronts us as a single realm, personal and collective, inner and outer, archetypical and institutional. It is the experience of the *unity* of the forces of fragmentation, and not religious obscurantism, that requires us to acknowledge the Prince of demons and his kingdom of death."[8] The sentence after that refers to Walter's being "appalled, that I am speaking this way." He finds himself saying words that obviously could be misappropriated by understandings of the Bible that are objectifying, and he yet remains committed to understanding the reality that he is referring to, and therefore endorses a statement far from his "native tongue."

∽

For a number of years I knew that Walter was working on the question of what used to be called "the son of man" and what we can now call "the human being"—or, as a few of us heretics say, "one like a person." Whatever the phrase used, critical opinion informed by his book, *The Human Being*, understands that the usage speaks of a basic structure

7. Ibid., 104.
8. Wink, *Unmasking the Powers*, 68.

of humanity, linking individuals together by a common, spiritual reality. I was delighted when Walter took this project up, because it was very involving and complex, offering us a rich intersection for discussion whenever we met. When we crossed paths at meetings of "The Jesus Seminar" or the Society for Biblical Literature I knew that in the midst of these jamborees I could look forward to an actual conversation of substance about the New Testament, rather than an endless run of scuttlebutt about the politics of the field. An all too rare expectation.

Because I had long known that Walter goes for substance rather than scuttlebutt, I was not exactly astonished when he took his public leave of the hermeneutics of "The Jesus Seminar." Its members have sometimes reminded me of an enthusiastic automobile club whose younger members have convinced themselves they are moving very quickly on a racetrack, just on the evidence of the noise they make. But they are driving model T's of positivistic history, so their sound has not translated into speed or progress. But that is another story all together.

In his book *The Human Being,* Walter makes a move that on a basic level comes as a relief to his readers. The context of the times had made it necessary for him to commit himself early in his career to his analysis of the powers and their demonic permutations. But many of us were awaiting something more cheerful. And *The Human Being* is exactly that, because it takes the analysis of archetypes and then, through the reading of the Prophet Ezekiel, sees that the human being, also known as the son of man, is not only in God's image, but also that God is within that image.

Walter sees that Jesus' expression implies that God is human, offering an interplay between humanity and divinity that cannot be exhausted. He writes, "The Christological revelation centered in Jesus was that God desired to become incarnate in humanity." That's the way that we usually think of the incarnation, although Walter says it more crisply than most. But he goes on, "The anthropological revelation, not yet consummated, is that God has destined humanity, or at least has called it, to become human as God is Human."[9]

Walter justifies that stance because he is able to show that the former discussion of what is usually called the "son of man debate" has got itself caught up in false options. Typically, our approach has seemed

9. Wink, *The Human Being,* 259.

something like a multiple-choice examination. When Jesus referred to the son of man, was he talking about (a) himself, (b) everyone on the face of the earth, or (c) some kind of divine entity? Walter is saying with a few of us, "Hello, he can talk about all three at once, if he likes." The poetics of preaching in the idiom of the Kingdom of God is precisely the language that permits expression of the unity of self, humanity as a whole, and the human image in the divine. But then Walter goes beyond that to demonstrate that in this idiom we are confronting an archetype that addresses our transformation as human beings and *at the same time* the realization of God.

What is it like, as a New Testament scholar, to read Walter Wink? It is like listening to J. S. Bach's "Concerto for Two Violins," where the instruments resonate with one another. Bach designed much of that resonance, of course, but he also exploited the literal vibration that one violin can induce in another. Walter Wink has been about putting us in a relationship to the New Testament, so that we can feel its resonance within ourselves. Without that relationship there is no music in our work.

3

Walter Wink
and Hermeneutics

J. Harold Ellens

WALTER WINK IS A PROFESSOR AT AUBURN THEOLOGICAL SEMINARY
in New York City. His specialty and faculty discipline is Biblical
Interpretation. In this important world of very specialized scholarship
he has published an impressive spate of sturdy books, a number of
which have won prestigious awards. In 2002, Fortress Press brought out
a volume which is perhaps the crown of his creation, the fruit of his long
scholarly endeavor at understanding the Bible and sharing his insights
with us. That volume is entitled, *The Human Being: Jesus and the Enigma
of the Son of the Man*. It addresses what may well be the knottiest theological problem for both Christianity and the Second Temple Judaism
from which Christianity arose—namely, the problem of the meaning of
Jesus' apparent self-designation, The Son of Man.

Marcus Borg, of Jesus Seminar fame, declared that Wink's new
book is impressive, brilliant, passionate, powerful, and provocative. He
called it a remarkable integration of religion, psychology, politics, the
quest for Jesus, and our yearning for "The Human Being" that we see
in Jesus. He says that Wink and his new book fill us with a passion for
becoming truly human. There is good reason for Borg so to praise this
work. Wink's objective in this volume is to recover the true meaning
of the humanity of Jesus, which was to a large extent appreciated by
the Jesus movement and by the earliest Christian church. Yet by the
mid-second century this was being eclipsed as the church became preoccupied with the question of the divinity of Jesus.

Amy-Jill Levine, professor of New Testament Studies at Vanderbilt, approves of Wink's undertaking, describing it as an admirable scholarly endeavor that conjoins rigorous historical-critical analysis of Son of Man traditions in ancient Judaism with sound reflections on philosophy, psychology, and mysticism. She sees in this new book rich insights into both the ancient exilic texts of Ezekiel and Daniel and the late first and early second century CE texts of the gospels. Levine thinks Wink leads us to a new understanding of Jesus within his own immediate context, thus recovering not only Jesus' humanness but also the ideal possibilities of our humanness. The book is a lens through which we can discover what it means to be human, regardless of whether we agree with Wink's personal theological perspective or religious identity.

Wink's previous books alerted us to the powerful impact this one could be expected to have. He edited *Peace is the Way: Writings on Nonviolence from the Fellowship of Reconciliation*, as well as *Homosexuality and Christian Faith: Questions of Conscience for the Churches*. He has written a dozen books, including his prize-winning series on "the Powers."[1] In addition, we have from his pen such worthies as *Violence and Nonviolence in South Africa*; *The Bible in Human Transformation*; *John the Baptist in the Gospel Tradition*; and *Transforming Bible Study*.

In *The Human Being*, Wink offers us seventeen chapters organized in six parts, plus three appendixes, a glossary, and appropriately detailed indexes. Fortress has packaged it in a genuinely attractive binding. The message of the book is organized around the following six themes: 1) The Original Impulse of Jesus; 2) The Anthropic Revelation: The Human Being; 3) The Human Being: Pre-Easter Sayings; 4) The Human Being: Post-Easter Sayings; 5) The Human Being in Jewish Mysticism and Gnosticism; and 6) Results and Conclusions.

Wink takes his title from Albert Schweitzer's famous book, *The Quest for the Historical Jesus*, in which Schweitzer says that "the historical Jesus will be to our time a stranger and an enigma."[2] A number of enigmatic themes are developed in detail under a rich selection of

---

1. This series includes: 1) *The Powers That Be: Theology for a New Millennium*, 2) *Engaging the Powers: Discernment and Resistance in a World of Domination*; 3) *Unmasking the Powers: The Invisible Forces That Determine Human Existence*; 4) *Naming the Powers: The Language of Power in the New Testament*; and 5) *When the Powers Fall: Reconciliation in the Healing of Nations*.

2. Schweitzer, *The Quest of the Historical Jesus*, 399.

chapter headings: "The Human Being in the Quest for the Historical Jesus," "The Enigma of the Son of the Man," "Feuerbach's Challenge," "Other Biblical and Extrabiblical Reference to the Human Being up to 100 CE," "Jesus and the Human Being," "Jesus and the Messianic Hope," and "The Human Being: Catalyst of Human Transformation." Six additional chapters cover the son of man in apocalypticism, and two highlight the concept in mysticism.

Wink's argument may be summarized readily and clearly, and I undertake it here with deep appreciation for him and his book. A good way to begin is by quoting the first paragraph of *The Human Being*, which sets the course for his entire discussion.

> "The son of the man" is the expression Jesus almost exclusively used to describe himself. In Hebrew the phrase simply means "a human being." The implication seems to be that Jesus intentionally avoided honorific titles, and preferred to be known simply as "the man," or "the human being." Apparently he saw his task as helping people become more truly human.[3]

Wink's approach to this issue is in the spirit of trying to disclose the original truths of Christianity and express them in modes that speak to interested folk in our day and feed our quest for both self-understanding and transcendental insights. This is crucial, he thinks, because the tradition of the faith has been so badly twisted throughout history that it is difficult for persons, and for the church, clearly to see and do what Jesus had in mind. It is virtually impossible to discern any longer what he was really up to. This perplexity is largely a legacy of the Imperial Church, established by Constantine in the fourth century, and structured by the creeds and episcopal program of authority in the fourth and fifth centuries. Douglas John Hall recently addressed this problem in his important little book, *The End of Christendom and the Future of Christianity*, in a way most congenial to Wink's concern here.[4] Wink formulates the issues succinctly:

> . . . anti-Semitism, collaboration with oppressive political regimes, the establishment of hierarchical power arrangements in the churches, the squeezing of women from leadership positions, the abandonment of radical egalitarianism, and the rule of pa-

3. Wink, *The Human Being*, xi.
4. Hall, *The End of Christendom and the Future of Christianity*.

triarchy in church affairs. Those of us who are to varying degrees disillusioned by the churches feel that it is not only our right but our sacred obligation to delve deeply into the church's records to find answers to these legitimate and urgent questions:

- Before he was worshiped as God incarnate, how did Jesus struggle to incarnate God?

- Before he became identified as the source of all healing, how did he relate to, and how did he teach his disciples to relate to, the healing Source?

- Before forgiveness became a function solely of his cross, how did he understand people to have been forgiven?

- Before the Kingdom of God became a compensatory after-life or a future utopia adorned with all the political trappings that Jesus resolutely rejected, what did he mean by "the kingdom"?

- Before he became identified as Messiah, how did he relate to the profound meaning in the messianic image?

- Before he himself was made the sole mediator between God and humanity, how did Jesus experience and communicate the presence of God?[5]

Wink has undertaken this work confident he could find enough data in scripture and in history to make a significant contribution to a number of the issues involved here, especially (1) to focusing the authentic memory of Jesus of Nazareth; and (2) to creating "a new myth, "the myth of the human Jesus."[6]

Wink acknowledges from the outset that recovering the historical Jesus "as he really was" is impossible. What he thinks he can discern is what Jesus intended us to understand by "the reign of God" he was proclaiming. Wink thinks the center of that issue is a new way of thinking about what it means to be a human being before the face of God. *This,* he contends, is what Jesus meant to convey by his self-designation as The Son of The Man. The crucial thing about Jesus is not his divinity but his humanness. His divinity is precisely his special way of being hu-

5. Wink, *The Human Being*, 2.
6. Ibid., 3.

man. "The Human Being means what Jesus was, and how he was, and what his process of individuation was."[7]

Wink's argument is very persuasive, and if we take this line of thought seriously, it will land us in something like this mystery: "God is Human and we are to become like God."[8] The quest for humanness is the hunger and search for becoming an individuated human person with the personal characteristics of God. These characteristics have to do with cherishing others in a way that champions the unique, precious, and inherent qualities and potential of each human person, resisting with courage and aggressive vigor all forces and powers intending to devalue, denigrate, and degrade human personhood in any and every human being.

The key biblical narrative and metaphor upon which Wink bases his argument is the manner in which the term, son of man, is used in Ezekiel and Daniel. He urges us to recognize that the man in Ezekiel who calls Ezekiel a son of man, is the "Ancient of Days" who sits on the throne; in Daniel 7:13 and following, the son of man is raised up to this throne, introduced to the Ancient of Days, and exalted. This enthroned figure, Wink argues, is The Ultimate Human, namely God, by whom the son of man is exalted. We are to be his sons and daughters—authentic human beings after the model of the Human. Following Wink, a sound Christological formula should look something like this:

> God as the Human One
> Ezekiel as the son of that Human One
> Jesus as the son of that Human One
> Hence Jesus as the Son of God, the Human One.[9]

The intent of Wink's work is reflected in a paragraph from Frederick Borsch, one of the scholars who made a valiant effort to uncover the meaning of the Son of Man title or phrase in the Synoptic Gospels.

> Jesus . . . was not content to preach about a myth; he had to discover how that myth related to the actualities of his own life and those of his disciples. In everyday situations as well as in his entire ministry he was engaged in the process of forcing the myth up against the hard facts of life, making what truths it

7. Ibid., 253.
8. Ibid., 257.
9. Ibid., 256.

held to become real and alive . . . . Without the myth, Jesus
might not have been able to accept the cross; without the cross
we would never have known how much truth lay beyond even
the revelatory powers of this myth.[10]

Since the publication of this book, the interchanges by Wink and many
of his colleagues have been tough-minded and hard-headed. Clearly the
debate has been driven by a deep respect for Wink's work; a profound
interest in the truth about Jesus, about history, and about theology; and
unusual scholarly grace and goodwill.[11]

10. Borsch, *The Son of Man in Myth and History*, 404.

11. I had the privilege of inviting five internationally notable scholars to a special
book session at the Society of Biblical Literature Convention in Toronto in November
2002: Alan Segal of Barnard College and Columbia University, Dale Burkett of Louisiana
State University, Jack Miles of the Getty Museum and the University of Southern
California, Gabriele Boccaccini of the University of Michigan, and Wayne Rollins of
Assumption College and Hartford Seminary. Each agreed to present critique, appreciation, and scholarly response to *The Human Being: Jesus and the Enigma of the Son of the
Man*. Those scholarly critiques were assembled, and Walter Wink was invited to provide
his written response to all of them. A very inadvertent, certainly serendipitous, and, I
must say, wholly delightful, encounter between me and Charles Henderson, on a shared
taxi ride in Toronto, led to his invitation to publish the work in *Cross Currents* (Ellens,
"Six critics").

4

Walter Wink
and Theology

Henry Mottu

I CAME TO KNOW WALTER WINK IN THE EARLY SEVENTIES WHEN HE
was teaching New Testament at Union Theological Seminary. I arrived
from Geneva, Switzerland, with little knowledge of English; yet I had
been invited to teach European philosophy of religion (Feuerbach,
Marx, Kant, Hegel). I remember how much Walter and other friends
helped me and my family find our way in a foreign setting. Still today,
it is somehow strange for me to think of these years and to realize that
New York City is in some way my second home.

"Historical biblical criticism is bankrupt"

Around that same time James Cone had been appointed as a visiting
professor, along with Rubem Alves from Brazil, and so we often came
together to discuss different matters like biblical exegesis, black theology,
Marxism, etc. This was a revolutionary time! A lively discussion arose
in this context around Walter's famous affirmation: "Historical biblical
criticism is bankrupt." I can remember exactly the context in which this
startling sentence was first uttered and then recorded in the small book,
*The Bible in Human Transformation: Toward a New Paradigm for Biblical
Theology.*

What was the author's intention behind this phrase? My own interpretation, more than thirty years later as a part of the *Wirkungsgeschichte*
of this statement, is that Wink deeply wanted to return biblical exegesis
back into God's hands. The Bible belongs to God—not to us, not to a
sequestered scholarship, not even to the Church. It speaks for itself, and

we have to listen to the Word that speaks in, with, and underneath the words of the Bible. And so Walter's pronouncement takes its place along Karl Barth's famous statement in the Preface of his second *Römerbrief*: "The historical critics must be *more critical!*"[1]

So I guess you could say that my understanding of Wink's project is one of "an old leftist Barthian," as one of my students recently called me. I think that Walter was *not* saying that scholarly *critique* is no longer needed. (A non-critical Christianity could be very dangerous indeed, as we all know.) And I don't think that Wink wanted to dislocate faith from historical scrutiny. What he did want to do was to warn against a scholarship separated from the lived experience and from the engaged faith of readers. For, look at the subtitle of this book: "Toward a New Paradigm *for Biblical Theology*"! The second part of that phrase has tended to be forgotten. Wink's contribution has been his fight for a renewed theological exegesis and for an original basis for building it—which is so very much needed still today.

The Principalities and Powers

In the fall of 1970, Paul Lehmann, Walter, and I gave a seminar on *Apocalypse and Revolution: Explorations in Iconoclastic Theology*, and I remember how Walter, in these years, was rediscovering the importance of apocalypticism and its relevance for a political theology today. We were not alone, and I could mention many names, among which would be Jacques Ellul in France and Amos Niven Wilder in the States. In particular I should mention Paul Lehmann and his *Politics as Transfiguration*; Lehman was my mentor at UTS and was almost the only prominent white theologian who was engaging black theology.

All of us were intrigued by the images of the Apocalypse, which we tried to translate through a wide variety of approaches—psychoanalytic, political, hymnical-liturgical, artistic. Our attempt to include within theology the so-called human sciences—the sociology of knowledge, psychoanalysis, political philosophy, etc.—emerged from our efforts to better understand the strangeness of those images. Wink had rightly sensed that a mere *rationalistic* theology could not meet our understanding of human destiny, so he tried to complement reason by including

---

1. Translation mine. In the English edition, the text reads: "The critical historian needs to be more critical." Barth, *The Epistle to the Romans*, 9.

the deeper elements of our nature (and here Tom Driver's influence was crucial).

It was courageous, and even prophetic, on Walter's part to tackle anew the classic problem of the interpretation of the Principalities and Powers from the New Testament. How could we make sense of these alien figures? His trilogy has been for me a lasting subject of reading, meditating and nurturing. How amazing is this approach that combines exegesis and psychology, theology and politics, piety and philosophy!

Theologically speaking, his focus on the Powers had the ability to dislodge Christianity from a mere religious humanism, to displace a merely anthropocentric view of humanness and to recapture a sensitivity for the world as *cosmos*—for the things still *unknown* to us. This is what we call in our philosophical French jargon: *le sens de l'altérité* (the sense for/of otherness). The early church of course understood this:

> We believe in one God, the Father, the Almighty,
> maker of heaven and earth,
> of all that is, seen *and unseen*.

Naming the Powers, unmasking them, and engaging the Beast *is* our new paradigm for biblical studies, and beyond that, for our theological *existence* today.

God Is the Intercessor

In lectures and speeches I have often used the acclaimed sixteenth chapter of the trilogy's third volume: "Prayer and the Powers."[2] I not only use this, but depend upon it for inspiration in my own prayer life, for indeed "God is the Intercessor!" This chapter has been often reprinted separately. I remember that when I was in Yaoundé, Cameroon, to give lectures there, Paul Frelick's wife Elenor said of this passage, "Every line of this text has helped me." (Indeed, prayer in Africa can replace the Internet, television, and cellphone!) Walter has not taught us *how* to pray (we must do this ourselves, within the resources of our own cultures), but Walter has taught us *why* to pray. "Intercession," he writes, "is spiritual defiance of what is, in the name of what God has promised."[3] God's promise stands prior to our efforts and prior to our language.

---

2. Wink, *Engaging the Powers*, 297–317.
3. Ibid., 298.

This is something that Walter's interpreters have not always under-stood—that Walter Wink has developed a *theocentric* understanding of prayer. Before we pray, God through His Spirit *is* already in travail in us. "We do not know how to pray . . . but God's Spirit within us is actually praying for us in those agonizing longings ["groans"] which cannot find words" (Romans 8:26–27). *We do not know*: this is the mark of a true theologian.

Wink is at his best when explaining Romans 8 to us today. Here is perhaps the most beautiful chapter of the Paul's writing, and Walter's commentary on it is a meditation on Pascal and Augustine, as well: "You would not seek me, had you not already found me." Only in prayer do we truly acknowledge that God is present. True theology is never a primary, but always a secondary act—not of creation, but of *recognition*. And in just this regard, "the message is clear: History belongs to the in-tercessors, who believe the future into being."[4] This message has crossed the oceans, the languages and cultures.

Spirituality and Politics

We should all be grateful that Walter Wink belongs to the rare breed of American theologians who, despite the easy path into conformity with the *Zeitgeist*, have constantly refused to separate spirituality from poli-tics and politics from spirituality. For just as the political world needs to be healed, the religious world needs to be concretized, and what strikes me in the trilogy on the Powers is its author's attempt to search out a principle that could reunite what Paul Ricœur once called short-term relationships (*relations courtes*) with long-term relationships (*relations longues*). In the trilogy's first volume, Wink has this remarkable note: "The goal of personal individuation becomes inseparable from the goal of cosmic reconciliation."[5]

An individualistic and moralistic Christianity has no future. A cos-mic faith is what we need, inspired through a new language and even, perhaps, new institutions. Wink's trilogy offers some balanced thinking about just this. For institutions always have (he says) two dimensions: an outer dimension, which is visible in human history, and an inner dimension, which is spiritual in its impact. These are never absolutely

4. Ibid., 299.
5. Wink, *Naming the Powers*, 147.

distinct, and they are both necessary and dangerous. Christians have to pray (and to fight) *on both levels*, spiritual and political. Every institution has its own "angel," as the Apocalpyse puts it, and our vocation is to be alert to this spiritual dimension, while not leaving behind our daily task within history.

The fact that Wink has performed this task with *hypomonè*, to use again a word of the last book of the Bible—with absolute intransigence, relentless firmness—remains his greatest contribution to me as an exegete and as a friend.

5

Walter Wink
and Pedagogy

Sharon H. Ringe

THE WORK THAT WALTER WINK BEGAN HAS SET THE AGENDA FOR
at least a generation of students and teachers of Bible.[1] Though Walter
might not use the quaint language of Charles Wesley—that God would
"Unite the two so long disjoined, knowledge and vital piety"—this has
been Walter's own working aim throughout his career. "Knowledge" in
this case would refer to the valuable but often poorly directed tools of
critical biblical scholarship, and "vital piety" would include not only
prayer ("history belongs to the intercessors"[2]), but also the pursuit of
justice and peace that is an earthly reflection of the sovereign project of
God.

I want to reflect in particular on how that prayer/hymn is lived
out in his contribution to two areas dear to all biblical scholars (in
terms that make normal people's eyes glaze over): methodology and
pedagogy. Before he published his ground breaking *The Bible in Human
Transformation*, we were taught that biblical scholarship had to be as
"objective" as we could make it. Who we were as human beings, what
our life's story and social and historical context had taught us, and the
commitments to which our faith had led us were to be left outside the
study door. We honed our skills in the various tools of historical criticism

1. I am grateful for this opportunity to join in honoring my dear friend Walter
Wink on his retirement from Auburn Seminary. I was privileged to have Walter as a
teacher and advisor from the moment I began my Masters of Divinity at Union until
the day I defended my doctoral dissertation. Regardless of whose signature ended up on
the dotted line, I am proud to claim my identity as Walter's student.

2. Wink, *Engaging the Powers*, 299.

in an effort to get beneath the veneer of later church doctrine, to what the biblical books *really* meant in their own periods of origin. By that, we hoped to arrive at a conclusion recognized as valid by any scholar in our discipline, and we argued vociferously with any who happened to differ over how we reached that conclusion. After we had done that, our task as biblical scholars was finished, and we had only to lob our result over to colleagues in homiletics, ethics, and other fields of the theological curriculum, so that these results could be "applied" somehow to the concerns of our present age.

Pedagogically, the corresponding style for biblical studies was the information-driven and highly authoritarian model of the academic lecture. As one of my students summarized it, "It's the 'I talk, you listen' model—and if you finish before I do, raise your hand." We as faculty believed that we had the correct meanings of the texts, and our obligation was to transmit them to our students and to defend them to our colleagues.

As a pastor Walter had learned the futility of both of those projects. The spirit of the age and the press of the historical crises that marked it were calling into question all authoritarian models, in the parish or in the classroom, as well as everywhere else in society. And Walter recognized, well ahead of most of his colleagues in the biblical guild, that the objective scholarship we were taught to value was both impossible to achieve and unhelpful to apply in the living communities that turned to the Bible as the ground of their faith and practice.

Walter recognized that the social chasms created by such events as the civil rights movement and the war in Vietnam demanded a different kind of involvement from us as scholars. He affirmed, in that now famous opening sentence of *The Bible in Human Transformation,* that the tools of biblical criticism were still valuable, but the enterprise in which they were used had gone "bankrupt." Not surprisingly, Walter caught all sorts of flak from the guild of biblical scholars for making that observation. In the intervening years, however, countless others have arrived at the same conclusion. Having learned from Walter's experience not to comment directly on the emperor's wardrobe, we found other ways to say it. We spoke of the need for "contextual readings" or "the view from below," for example, as we mined the resources of the critical disciplines for tools that could serve our new projects. For some, those projects have taken us in the direction of social world analysis, or toward a literary criticism rooted in aesthetics and the arts, rather than analysis of the history of composition of biblical texts. Others of us find our attention drawn more to the social locations of contemporary readers than to further plumbing of the ancient texts. We find ourselves learning to use ethnography and other social sciences to find the human stories embedded in literary language. And we have learned to ask about the consequences of the biblical texts for the various members of human communities who either experienced those texts being transformed into beacons of hope, or suffered those texts being weaponized into vehicles of submission.

Walter's work has joined depth psychology (especially refracted through the lens of the Guild for Psychological Studies) and split-brain theory with traditional biblical scholarship and social-justice ministries, to unfold into his program of Bible study for human transformation. Walter's method of Bible study was what today we would call interactive. It can be described as "Socratic"—as long as we do not mean some of the artificial questions of Socrates' pedagogy in Platonic dialogues.

To put it another way, Walter insisted on a relationship to the text that I would call "iconic." Just as in the Orthodox tradition one meditates on an icon, studying it and gazing at its components until it turns the tables and begins to gaze back, interpreting the worshipper—so in this way of doing Bible study we analyze the text with every tool at our disposal, until we find that it has begun to interpret us. It interprets each of us—teacher/guide and student alike. For this purpose, Walter incorporated the arts, not just to "illustrate" an idea, but to serve as a critical lens for our own actual experience. He insisted that we "feel our way into a text" or "hunch our way to a solution of a problem," in a context where many of us had learned not to feel at all, but to respond instead with the oxymoronic statement, "well, I think I feel . . ." In a historical moment when the political clamor was calling us to rapid-fire external action, Walter's methodological revolution called us back into our own depths, to realize how our own individual unconscious was shaping our actions and even influencing the very political and social crises we sought, often unsuccessfully, to address.

That emphasis on the personal and the individual was a crucial note in the cacophony of public crises through which we were living. We needed that grounding. What Walter was doing both before and after the landmark publication of *The Bible in Human Transformation* touched a chord in many of us. Even those of us who resisted it mightily had to come to terms with its power to open up texts, to enable new insights, and to change lives.

∽

When I began to teach, both as a tutor at Union and at the Methodist Theological School in Ohio, I followed what I had learned from Walter and from the Guild for Psychological Studies. In reflecting on my own teaching practices in order to prepare this essay, though, I have become aware of how those practices have changed. I say this, not in defiance or rebellion, but in tribute to the integrity of Walter's teaching. He never suggested that he wanted clones. Rather, he wanted students who were also committed to the project of human transformation in engagement with the biblical text, wherever that project took us.

So here I assume a posture appropriate to a celebration of retirement. I want to stand between memory and hope—between reflecting on what Walter has done in his career and looking toward where that might be leading us in the present and into the future. As one way to do that, I want to reflect on some of the factors that have shaped and that continue to shape my own incarnation of that project, as one of Walter's students. It's both *what* he taught me, and *how* he taught me. It's the *questions* rather than the *answers*. (As Rilke said, ". . . be patient toward all that is unresolved in yourself, and learn to love the questions themselves."[3])

The participatory model of pedagogy itself has value beyond measure, both in the insights that evolve when a group labors together on a text, and in the empowerment of people as interpreters whose experience, ideas, and feelings are respected. The reality of large classes is the principal factor limiting my use of such a teaching model. In the introductory courses, we muddle along, with as much interaction as is possible in an amphitheater and with only the electronic "Blackboard" program to enable sustained group discussion. As a genuine technophobe, I am sure that it is only the challenge of Walter's dialogical model and my experience of its value that have pushed me to explore that technology. I am convinced that technology in the classroom has tremendous potential for good and for harm. On the one hand, it can enable "conversation" in contexts where it would be otherwise impossible and open a space for all to have a voice. On the other hand, it can re-center, if not the

---

3. Rilke, *Letters to a Young Poet*, 34–35.

single voice of a teacher's authority, at least the voices of the elites that have control of the electronic toys. That is of concern to me both in the microcosm of the classroom and in the global context within which our discipline is practiced.

When I studied with Walter, the issues and the demographic changes that came onto the stage with the women's movement were only beginning to appear. So I cannot credit (or blame) Walter for the feminist directions in which my own scholarship has moved in the intervening years. But I go back to the questions he taught me to love—taking seriously the hunches that old answers were not working, and finding courage to say to ecclesiastical and academic stars alike, "That text is a text of terror." If a text has been used to warrant the abuse of women, or children, or gays in communities I know, in order to *understand* the text, not just in order to preach on it today, one must ask how those groups in the communities of the origin and transmission of the text would have experienced its power. Obviously not all feminist scholars were shaped by Walter's work, but I certainly was, and I found from that work both the means and the courage to stay with the work that we have needed to do.

What I have just said about feminism is echoed in the tectonic shifts brought to biblical studies from the Two Thirds World—what have been called "voices from below" or "voices from the margin." Just as the pursuit of feminist concerns in biblical studies (as in other disciplines) has been abetted by the entry of large numbers of women into the guild of scholars, so also other shifts in demographics, or at least awareness, have introduced other changes. Obviously people in the African diaspora, Latino/as, and those in the Asian diaspora in Europe and North America—like people in Asia, Africa, Latin America, Oceania, and the Caribbean—have been interpreting the Bible for years. However, the insights arising from the intersection of their realities and cultures with the biblical texts have only quite recently popped up on the radar screen of the biblical guild. But the numbers of those scholars gaining access to the discussions of the various Societies for Biblical Literature are increasing, and the freshness and importance of their insights cannot be denied. Bit by bit, *poco a poco*, we are being taught about the Bible by those whose cultures and lifestyles are less removed from the realities from which those texts emerged.

Can we credit Walter for that? In one sense, of course, no. But in another sense, certainly yes. The reception Walter's work received from "the authorities" was a precursor to the struggles women, persons of color, and other persons from outside the arenas of power and control have experienced when we tried to speak the truth as we encountered it in our social locations. His emphasis on speaking from the circle of interpreters—a circle in which each voice and perspective is honored as part of the whole—prepared the way, I think (along with other social and cultural factors of our age), for the richly textured fabric that is the discipline of biblical studies today.

Finally, some people would dismiss "the posts"—post-modernism and postcolonialism—as simply the latest intellectual flavor-of-the-month in biblical scholarship. I am sympathetic to those who find post-modernism an ironic and somehow predictable development: as soon as groups historically excluded from debates over truth-claims found our way to the table, we learned that the table itself is a relic of *modernité passée!* But taken together—post-modernism's affirmation of the validity of a diversity of voices, coupled with postcolonialism's emphasis on the still-excluded voice of the "subaltern," and its critical analysis of the historical and continuing role of the colonial projects of human social systems and behaviors—the contribution of these disciplines to critical study of the Bible can be great indeed. After all, much of the Bible was shaped by the colonial projects in the Ancient Near East and the Roman Empire and by resistance and counter-voices to those projects. Hence, critical analysis of both colonial projects and currents of resistance is crucial to understanding the human meanings and consequences of the texts that many today call "holy." Furthermore, the appropriation of the Bible throughout the world has been guided by other colonial projects—political, economic, cultural, linguistic, academic, and certainly religious—that have struggled to silence views and texts that would call those projects into question.

Walter's work stands as a model of postcolonial criticism aimed at what I would call the "colonial project"—the hegemony of historical critical scholarship in the theological academy. In fact, I would even say that one of Walter's contributions to our discipline has been to demonstrate—even to incarnate—for us the postcolonial struggle that continues to challenge us and our communities, and continues to call us into the future.

6

Walter Wink
as Philosopher

D. Seiple

THE RENOWNED OLD TESTAMENT SCHOLAR BERNHARD ANDERSON reports to us that the ancient rabbis, disturbed over the account of Ezekiel's vision and the strange doctrines that might result from too wide a hearing of it, forbade the public reading of Ezekiel's opening chapter, and even stipulated that no persons under thirty years of age should read the book privately.[1] Times have obviously changed. I first met Walter Wink down at the Open Center in Soho, talking about his newly published book *The Human Being*,[2] which seeks to make the kind of sense out of Ezekiel's opening chapter that we all can understand. At the time, I did not understand where that encounter would take me, nor how much it would change my thinking on matters that, frankly, I thought I knew a great deal about already. I learned that I did not know nearly as much as I thought.

My appointed task here today is to offer some modest philosophical observations on Walter Wink's work. But even to mention the words "modesty" and "philosophy" in the same breath might strike some as rather odd, because philosophy has not typically been very modest. One could be more modest, after all, than to purport to offer rational insight into the very nature of reality—which is what philosophers have often been wont to do. Now Walter Wink is an exceedingly modest man, and I'm not sure he'd be comfortable being called a philosopher of that sort. But nevertheless, Walter does speak consistently, forcefully, and by

1. Anderson, *Understanding the Old Testament*, 433.
2. Seiple, "Review of Walter Wink, *The Human Being*."

now famously about what he calls the "Powers that Be," which seem to be reigning, currently but temporarily, in our very fallen world. Only a person who has a vivid enough sense of the real nature of things—a philosophical aspiration, after all—would be in a position to really say much about those principalities and powers.

So Walter's project is, among other things, philosophical. But I imagine that he suspects what many of us philosophers sometimes forget, which is that philosophy is an inherently limited discipline, with inevitable fissures and tensions and even inconsistencies, which are internal to any worthwhile philosophical system or project. These are left to other philosophers to identify. Since my assignment here is to speak the philosopher's voice, I shall attempt do just that—to uncover a logical tension in Walter's writing which I think points to a profound philosophical issue. It might even be the most profound philosophical issue of our time.

I perform this gentle task, much sobered after having once again spent much time these past weeks reconsidering what Walter has said, and along the way, I've had a humbling and startling realization. I've had to ask myself: what in the world have I been doing reading philosophy *instead* of reading this? This is good stuff—tension, fissures, and all. I can't speak about Walter's influence on the *profession* of philosophy nearly as well as I can about his influence on my own thinking *in* philosophy.

So let me begin by recalling that Walter has made a virtual career of contesting dominant paradigms, but he does not (like a few in the field these days) contest the general paradigm of Christian faith itself, and he is not about to abandon the faithful notion that a real and holy power is at work in our spiritual life. This points to one pervasive philosophical theme for him—that there are two sides of power, as Michel Foucault himself would put it. First, we find arrayed all around us the "invisible dimension" of disciplinary social forces—whose very naming reveals the vivid and often terrible impact they have upon us.[3] These principalities and powers, Walter declares, can truly be "named" as actual spirits. This is not merely metaphor! Walter calls them "real though unsubstantial" forces "having no existence apart from their concretions in the world of

---

3. Wink, *The Powers That Be*, 3.

things,"[4] and anyone who doubts that Walter is a philosopher should commit that quote to memory! These forces are not to be reified, but, as Aristotle might say of Plato's realities, neither are they to be reduced and razored away.

So—on the one hand, we have the Powers That Be. On the other hand, Walter rather bravely posits what some postmodernists disparagingly call a "binary distinction." For in addition to the principalities and powers we all normally experience, Walter also distinguishes an essentially different power—of non-violent love—and love for Walter is metaphysically transforming. Here is Jesus' "third way" between passivity and violence.[5] In an age of very welcome interfaith dialogue and increasingly prolific "post-Christian" references, and in a world going quickly to hell in a terrorist's handbasket, Walter proclaims the Christian gospel as "the most powerful antidote. . . that the world has ever known."[6] "And the same God who calls us to nonviolence gives us the power to carry it out."[7]

In this, Walter Wink has been steadfast over the years. He has stoutly resisted attempts to explain away or deconstruct this Other and Holy Power. His devastating critique of Morton Smith's "magician" theory of Jesus ministry,[8] which demolished that cantankerous thesis plank by shaky plank, culminated in unmasking Smith's real agenda—namely, a "systematic effort to undermine the very ground on which Christian faith exists."[9] Smith's agenda was not a welcome proposal, from Walter's point of view—not then, back in 1978, and true to form, on *this* point at least, Walter has not changed his mind since.

The irony of Smith's work, Walter suggested back then, was that its real consequence might be not the debunking of Christianity, but the recovery of its shamanistic, miraculous, and healing power—in "a new synthesis of spirit and nature."[10] In retrospect, it would certainly be stretching things to say that Morton Smith has really done that. It

4. Wink, *Naming the Powers*, 4.

5. Wink, "Neither Passivity Nor Violence," 210–24.

6. Wink, *The Powers That Be*, 62.

7. Ibid., 135.

8. Smith, *Jesus the Magician*.

9. Wink, "Jesus as Magician," 11.

10. Ibid., 14.

would be much less of a stretch to reflect upon the ways that Walter Wink has done that.

This project of synthesizing "spirit" and "nature" is a thoroughly philosophical project. Can it be done? Well, it hasn't been easy. When Walter began that project, it was not at all clear (to some) that he wasn't being as much of a curmudgeon as the Morton Smiths of his profession. The very first sentence of his groundbreaking little book on biblical criticism—*The Bible in Human Transformation* (1973), written for his colleagues at Union and elsewhere—was the startling announcement that "historical biblical criticism is bankrupt."[11] Now this seems hardly well-designed to win friends and influence the very people who have made careers in that field, and indeed Walter did not stay too long at Union Theological Seminary. But, as in so much else, Walter had the last laugh on that, and Union's loss was Auburn's gain—made all the more palatable by the fact that yea these many years he has been gracing the halls of both seminaries. Fortunately, this has meant that he's been a very present and available resource to scholars and students at Union, who have been impressed by the fact that so many of Walter's younger colleagues in the biblical field began believing that what he was saying, back in 1973, might actually be true!

True in what sense, though? There's a philosophical question! And here's where the tension shows up. Here is where the story gets rather complex. Here is the point of logical tension. (1) For on the one hand, Walter wants to explain the spirituality of being human in terms of philosophical anthropology—which is the Christian liberal's view about where to start doing theology (namely, with the experience of being human). As Schleiermacher,[12] and even Calvin himself insisted,[13] we know God through God's relation to the world we experience, and so it is at least arguable (though in Calvin's case, ambiguously so[14]) that philosophical anthropology is the natural place for scholars to look. And so Walter, in his typically provocative style, takes the heretical Ludwig

---

11. Wink, *The Bible in Human Transformation*, 1.

12. Schleiermacher, *The Christian Faith*, §50.

13. Calvin, *Institutes*, I, iii, 1.

14. Ibid., I, iv.

Feuerbach as his model, at one point, declaring that "we can relate to God as human beings because God is truly 'Human.'"[15]

This makes Walter an unabashed liberal humanist. And though it's a crucial detail that slips past the befogged polemics of right-wing apologetics, the fact is that not all humanists are reductively secular humanists, and Walter's project has been to make clear just how this can be so.

(2) So on the one hand, we have Walter's humanistic liberalism. On the other hand, though—and here's where the puzzling and complex tension enters the picture—Walter is skeptical of the disinterested, "objectivist" categories that were traditionally used to buttress liberal theological explanation. This is just what led him to offer a "new paradigm for biblical study" back in 1973—the idea that there are "unconscious ideological elements"[16] that affect the selection and interpretation of data, in the biblical field just as in any other field of study. This is so obvious nowadays that we can hardly imagine ourselves back in the old historical-critical mindset, and Walter, once again the provocateur, declares that this very notion of an "'objective view' is itself an oxymoron; every view is subjective, from a particular angle of vision."[17] Walter does not want to call himself an objectivist.

And here's the problem! For it appears to leave Walter (and us with him) in a troublesome quandary, I think, because Walter's whole project *presupposes* a framework of objectivity. The Hebrew account of the exodus, Ezekiel's vision of God's throne, the social conscience of the minor prophets—all these indicate that, in Walter's view at least, something *objective* happened in the formation of the Old Testament: Other myths had been written entirely from the standpoint of the oppressors; but for the first time in human history, God begins to be seen as identified with the victims of violence.[18] (We see here the trace of what postmodernists disapprovingly call a "metanarrative.") And recently Walter has proclaimed once again that "something 'objective' did happen to God, to Jesus, and to the disciples" which was a fact about historical con-

---

15. Wink, *The Human Being*, 42.

16. Wink, *The Bible in Human Transformation*, 12.

17. Wink, *The Human Being*, 7.

18. Wink, *The Powers That Be*, 84–85.

sciousness and "not just an assertion of faith."[19] Not just, in other words, subjective. Were this not so, there would be no real power in Jesus' third way. Power is itself an objective category.

So what's to be done about this? That's what I've been trying to figure out. And in fact I'm not at all convinced that Walter's project is *deeply* inconsistent at this point—I suspect that the inconsistency is only at the rhetorical level. But even the appearance of inconsistency just sticks in the gut of any philosopher—which is one reason I've been reading this stuff so frenetically. There is more work to be done—a fact that keeps us scholars happily busy.

But I think that Walter calls upon us not to miss the forest for the footnotes. There is much more than a scholarly challenge for us here. Even scholars, after all, live in the real world of The Powers That Be. And in such a world—in the face of the suprahuman disciplinary Powers arrayed against us—Walter reminds us that the activity of prayer and of spiritual discernment is indispensable, because unless we win the battle on the interior spiritual battlefield, before external battles are joined, we will become like the very ones we fight. Evil will have made us over into its likeness. And in that case, we won't even know we've lost. We'll think we've actually won. Therein lies much of the sad part of the Christian legacy. And in his warnings against this, we are blessed to have the happy legacy of Walter Wink.

19. Wink, *The Human Being*, 152–53.

7

Walter Wink
and Peace Theology

Ted Grimsrud

A FEW YEARS AGO, I HEARD THE FOLKSINGER RICHIE HAVENS IN concert. Prior to one of his songs, he said that he wished he didn't feel he had to perform one particular song—not because it wasn't a good song, but because he wishes we could come to a point where it would no longer be relevant. But we have not made it to that point yet. So he proceeded with a passionate rendering of that anti-war song, "Lives in the Balance."

Maybe we could say the same thing about Walter Wink's theological analysis of nonviolence, and especially what he calls "the myth of redemptive violence." It would be nice to say that our world had changed so much since *Engaging the Powers* came out in 1992 that the book's powerful articulation of peace theology had lost much of its relevance. Were it only so.

If anything, Walter's work on peace versus violence is more relevant than when he first articulated it. I say this with gratitude for the brilliance and farsightedness of this work, but also with great sorrow that our society and the broader world have, if anything, become even more in thrall to the powers of domination. However, if the need continues, we may be grateful that we have Walter's work—just as Richie Havens expressed gratitude for Jackson Brown's "Lives in the Balance."

The term "peace theology" has been used in recent years for theological reflection that places at the center of its concern a vision for opposition to warfare and other forms of violence, and for alternative strategies of conflict resolution and resistance communities, to counter

45

our world's trust in redemptive violence. A very short, eclectic list of recent examples of such peace theology might include John Howard Yoder, *The Politics of Jesus*; J. Denny Weaver, *The Nonviolent Atonement*; Jack Nelson-Pallmeyer, *Jesus against Christianity*; Timothy Gorringe, *God's Just Vengeance*; Gil Baillie, *Violence Unveiled*; Rita Nakashima Brock and Rebecca Parker, *Proverbs of Ashes*; Christopher Marshall, *Beyond Retribution*; Howard Zehr, *Changing Lenses*; Gordon Kaufman, *In Face of Mystery*; and Stanley Hauerwas, *The Peaceable Kingdom*.

Walter's *Engaging the Powers* ranks at the very top of any such list. Every fall semester, when I introduce my undergraduate students to *Engaging the Powers,* I am always gratified by the excitement it generates. I believe Walter has helped set the agenda for peace theology for years to come. Among his many important insights, I mention just four that continue to engage us:

1) *His description of the continuing revolution in our worldview.* He helps us understand what worldviews are, how much they shape how we perceive the world around us, and how we must rethink our commitment to the *modern* worldview if we hope truly to be able to appropriate biblical insights in our work for human well-being. He helps us see how many characteristics of our modern, materialistic worldview reinforce domination—not least the tendency to view the world as constituted of discrete, autonomous entities. The failure to see how all things are interconnected underwrites much violence toward other humans beings and the natural world.

2) *Walter's invention of the useful term "domination system" to help us understand our present context.* This is obvious in the militarism of the United States, which finds justification in the ever-more-violent efforts to dominate others in the world—most clearly right now in Iraq and Afghanistan. However, all kinds of dynamics in our lives reflect the domination dynamic—from the approach to nature, which draws upon the familiar language of pioneers "conquering" the wilderness, to the spread of global capitalism. His profound analysis of the role of the Powers in human culture helps make sense of why our structures, with their reliance on the "myth of redemptive violence," are so destructive of human well-being. One of the great mysteries of modernity is how so many human efforts to bring about well-being have resulted in misery and injustice. Even well-intentioned people so often end up causing damage rather than healing with their efforts "to do good," and even

more troubling, people with less-than-good intentions all too often end up being elevated into positions of power. Walter helps us see that human institutions, in a sense, have "minds of their own" that all too often twist even the best of intentions to their own will.

3) *Walter's keen sense of empowerment and hope.* As we break free from the illusions of the domination system, we may be freed to recognize the biblical confession that the powers are not only corruptible ("fallen"), but are also the originally good creations of God. They are, in other words, redeemable. He provides us with a powerful basis for affirming human beings, our structures, and the wider world as "good" and as capable of transformation. Simply being disillusioned with the domination system itself is extraordinarily powerful in undermining its power, because so much of our bondage is self-imposed through our believing in the system. When our beliefs change, our innate goodness may assert itself and transformation may result.

4) *Walter's biblically-based vision of a domination-free order, grounded in the life and teaching of Jesus.* In his positive vision, Walter provides a vivid sense of a possibility that transcends even his indispensable critique of the domination system. Walter thoroughly demonstrates that violence is antithetical to the vision Jesus gives us of genuinely authentic human living. And he provides us with a practical outline for some creative responses to conflict, which includes in particular the art of learning from our enemies and which must be based upon our own vital, transformed spirituality.

Walter helps us understand *both* the depths of our culture's core commitment to the way of violence *and* the depths of the gospel's presentation of a viable alternative to that way of violence. He makes a powerful case for the *practical* relevance for our world of Jesus' message of a domination-free order.

Walter has helped unlock a world of resources from the biblical tradition that are needed in our world today. And the task continues! Ray Gingerich and I edited a volume, with Fortress Press, entitled *Transforming the Powers: Peace, Justice and the Domination System.*[1] Walter has contributed two essays to that volume. His first, "The New Worldview: Spirit at the Core of Everything," expands and updates his analysis of the integral worldview he envisions. His second chapter,

1. Grimsrud and Gingerich, eds., *Transforming the Powers.* This volume emerged from a conference at Eastern Mennonite University in March 2000.

"Providence and the Powers," applies the Powers analysis to the vexingly perennial problem of evil.

Other contributors follow in that same spirit. Expanding upon the work of Alasdair MacIntyre, Nancey Murphy applies a Winkian analysis to a critique of social thought, especially the fallen norms legitimated by social science and the value-laden "counter-theologies" implicit in that legitimation. Drawing on social theorist Ernest Becker, Dan Liechty enunciates how Walter's embrace of nonviolence negotiates the perils inherent in the unseen social forces and factors that so destructively shape us. Borrowing heavily from his own Mennonite tradition, Willard Swartley defends the tradition's stance of nonresistance ("non-retaliation") against the familiar charge of passivity, and envisions a more powerful "evil" than even Walter's more nuanced discussion incorporates.

So it is apparent, just from this one new volume, how widely applicable Walter's work has become. We see this in Glen Stassen's creative rereading of the Sermon on the Mount and his and his rethinking of Jesus' relation to the Old Testament prophets' views on social justice. We see this in Ray Gingerich's interpretation of the Reformation-era peasants' movement and in my own critique of the violence inherent in the worldview of western modernity. Ray and I are grateful to be able to offer this book as a tribute to Walter *and* as a means of continuing to build on the contribution Walter has thus far made.

8

Walter Wink
and Psychology

Hal Childs

DEAR WALTER,

I have decided to write you a letter because . . . well . . . this is personal, and I'll tell you why. You know how it goes in crime movies. The homicide detective says, "He was just another criminal until he touched my family. Now it's personal!" And what happens to us when we hear the words, "it's personal"? The intensity, the excitement, the passion, goes up several notches—we know we are in for a rule-breaking, crazy, wild ride; we know the criminal doesn't stand a chance! When I came to Union in 1972, I could have had a perfectly safe academic experience of graduate theological education. Walter, you were just another academic, until you touched my psyche. You made it personal, and it's never been the same since. Psychology has never been the same either.

My theme left me a bit stumped. What sort of impact are we talking about? Has your work been cited by psychologists? Not likely, but, I am curious. An exhaustive search, facilitated by Google, of the publications of the American Psychiatric Association and the American Psychology Association, produced zero hits of Walter Wink footnotes or bibliographic references. Actually, I just made that Google thing up, but it wouldn't surprise me in the least if this were the case. So, how am I going to evaluate your impact on psychology?

I want to reframe the images from our working title, "The Impact of Walter's Work on the Discipline of Psychology." The word "discipline" is related to "disciple," and "disciple" is our translation of the Greek word, *mathētēs*, which is related to the word "mathematics." In the ancient world, training in mathematics was fundamental. A disciple is a student, or an apprentice, who undergoes training at the hand of the fundamentals. Therefore, instead of "discipline," I will think in terms of "apprentice" of psychology.

"Psychology" is another image composed of two Greek words I know you are familiar with, *psyche* and *logos*. As familiar as these words are, let me say this, *psyche* equals soul, which can just as well equal life itself. For as Carl Jung was fond of saying, "The psyche is not in us, we are in the psyche." Psyche does have her own logic, but the notion of being an "apprentice of psyche"—now, that is juicier and fresher, it pulsates and challenges.

And, the image of your "work," what is that? Your many books and articles? Your many workshops? Well, yes, but that is the tip of the iceberg. The real "work," I will venture to say, is the *opus* of your life, the way you and psyche have wrestled, argued, shouted and whispered, and made love together, and, as a result, transformed each other, because, like Jacob, you would not let go until you were blessed—until you achieved the consciousness that psyche desired and needed you to be. Of course, consciousness has its price, and the wounding along the way richly textures the identity, your deep personhood, so hard-won.

One more word, "impact"—here's a word with force, muscle, penetration. But how can you impact psychology if you haven't been impacted yourself by psyche? My new working title is, "The Impact of Walter's Apprenticeship to Psyche on Walter and Psychology."

I find particularly delightful, and decisive, your own story of one of your first encounters with psyche—and, most especially, how she came in through the back door of your body:

> One of the early exercises in the first seminar I attended at the Guild for Psychological Studies in 1971 was to take the story of the Healing of the Paralytic in Mark 2:1–12 and internalize it by making in clay my own inner paralytic. I had a Ph.D. and a prestigious academic appointment; I "had" no paralytic. Life was careening along just fine, I thought. But to be a good sport I tried it. Shutting my eyes as they suggested, I let my hands have their way. After a period of time had passed, I looked to see what my hands had done. They had made a beautiful bird—with a broken wing! I am no artist, and was simply astonished that my hands had done this. More significant still, I suddenly knew precisely what that broken-winged bird was in me: an atrophied

feeling function. Thus began the task of recovering my capacity
to feel that was to last, in earnest, for the next eight years.[1]

Wait a minute. That was 1971. Isn't the Guild for Psychological
Studies in California? You were teaching in New York City. Weren't you
supposed to go east, "young man," to Germany for advanced biblical
studies, and bring back a briefcase full of footnotes? But no, psyche se-
duces us off the beaten path, and sends us out into marginal, unknown,
sometimes wacky places—not unlike that filthy, dark, out-of-the-way
stable, that comes around every Christmas. We never know where,
or when, the amazing birth will surprise us and change our life in the
process.

You may have thought you were being a "good sport," but I believe
that when you closed your eyes you were embarking on an adventure
and showing great courage—you took the plunge. To allow the clay bird
with the broken wing to form herself, to recognize the wounded feeling
function, and to accept as vocation the need to develop your own capacity for feeling, well, that reminds me . . . is this not like that other wild
bird, plunging at a baptism (was that bird wounded?), embodying a call
to live out something that had not yet been lived?

Carl Jung has said that development of one's personality is a vocation, and the creation of consciousness is a contemporary form of
incarnation. By accepting the call of the wounded bird as a personal
divine imperative, you wove together psychology and theology in your
own being, transforming each.

The really shocking thing is that you did not rest satisfied with
your own personal "enlightenment," but you brought the clay back to
Union Theological Seminary. You could have come back and handed
out a bibliography on Carl Jung, but you did one better—you handed
us, your students, the clay, the crayons, the paint brushes, and essentially
said, "Now that we have read this text with our intellects, go and allow
psyche to work her magic, see what will appear," and you sent us into
the darkness of our experience. I still remember vividly the first painting I made of my inner paralytic in your class on Mark in 1973. That
image provided much grist for personal inner work, and had profound
implications for my stance in society. Your impact on psychology was
to not allow it to remain in the academy, or simply in the intellect, but

1. Wink, "Write What You See," 7.

to bring her as psyche, as transformative power, directly into the lives of others because she had come so directly into your life.

You changed psychology by forcing us to see that psyche is not an individualistic subjectivism, something only inside our skin, but that truly, psyche is a social field within which we all live.

Because of who you are, and the tensions within your own being, you had to articulate, and to live, the fact that psyche is a field of shared social being. Not unlike how the kingdom of God is defined in the *Gospel of Thomas*: ". . . it is spread upon the earth and [we] do not see it;" and, ". . . it is within you and it is without you." No ambiguity here about the "kingdom" being inner or outer—it is both. I imagine that you long suffered a collision within you between three forces: (1) being an apprentice of psyche, (2) the great value of the biblical text and the teachings of Jesus, and (3) your commitment to social action and justice. Because these three areas had equal value in your own being, you could not reduce any to the other, but had to hold all three in tension, and forge a new synthesis. You did this by following a way that was your own, but which you could not control. At the time, it was sad that you did not gain tenure at Union. But, given the way your life work has gone, in looking back, this "accident" seems to have been, in your words, "providential."

(It is probably a very little-known fact that in 1999 Robert Funk and the Westar Institute installed you, along with seven other biblical colleagues, into the Order of D. F. Strauss. Perhaps a dubious distinction if academic tenure and security is your goal, and Strauss is the model. His historical and mythic view of the Gospels in the nineteenth century lost him his teaching post.)[2]

It is clear to me that with your work on the Powers, a deeply psychological work, you have wrestled psychology into a worldly, incarnational psychology by refusing to allow your analytical categories to separate into discrete disciplines. You insist on integrating psyche and world when you state:

> I am not arguing for an intrapsychic reductionism in which God, heaven, and the Powers are all conceived as mere projections and hence creations of our own unconscious psychic processes. Quite the reverse. The mind itself . . . is a microcosm of

2. See "The Order of D. F. Strauss," 27.

heaven, and thus our own interiority is continuous with and a clue to the interiority of reality itself.[3]

You also assert that, ". . . the goal of personal individuation becomes inseparable from the goal of cosmic reconciliation."[4] For you, the subjectivity of the person is conjoined with the within-ness of the world, and this is really the totality of psyche.

As I read you, psychology must be political. If the personal psychological task is to re-order the structures of power in the personal psyche, and free the personality from unjust internal domination, then the test of the true unity of psyche, your integrated view of person and world, is whether or not this new consciousness leads to political action and liberation. If not, then perhaps the personal psychological liberation is false, or stunted.

A final word about your most recent published work that engages the perennial biblical puzzle, "*the son of the man*." With this book you make a qualitative move, and allow the "clay" into your written scholarship. Having consciously abandoned the notion of a value-free objectivity in the historical quest for Jesus, you allow a different kind of objectivity into your work, and this is an objective subjectivity, a disciplined deeper subjectivity, something truly your own. You do not just employ psychology as one interpretive tool among others, you allow psyche to influence your writing. All prior interpreters have stumbled over this bizarre Greek neologism with the double definite article, "*the son of the man*." To this day there is no scholarly consensus on what this phrase could mean, and so it remains a wild and mysterious image at the heart of our Western spiritual traditions. Your book is an epochal turning point in this impasse and blazes a new path in a living interpretive process that combines thinking and feeling, head and heart. This ancient image, so far undomesticated by scholarly intellectualism, comes alive under the influence of your pen because you write not from the perspective of history, theology, or psychology, but from the vantage point of psyche. History, theology, myth, biblical criticism, and depth-psychology are all woven into your interpretation, but the real key to your understanding of *the son of the man* is the living psychic image, and the fierce vitality of psyche.

3. Wink, *Naming the Powers*, 141.
4. Ibid., 147.

In the end, Walter, it is the impact of psyche on you, desired or not, and your willingness to work with the impact, that is the source of your real impact on the discipline of psychology—this is a rich gift to the rest of us, and I am grateful for the privilege of being in the vicinity of the reverberations. May psyche continue to challenge you, and bless you with a deepening peace.

PART TWO

Testimonials *and* Toasts

9

A Prayer

Robert Raines

ALMIGHTY AND MOST GRACIOUS GOD,

 Creator of all that is holy, just and beautiful,

We praise You for bringing us together in this place

 To honor and celebrate Your servant, our friend Walter.

We thank You for all those in family and church who have nurtured his faith across the years,

 And for those who have supported his work,

 Especially June and the leaders of Auburn seminary.

We bless You for his blessed gifts to us and countless others,

 Of scholarship, teaching, writing, witness and friendship.

We honor his integrity, humility, and loyalty to the Gospel.

Thank You, O Lord, for the learning and pleasure of our conversations today.

Grant us, now, Your Spirit of joy as we toast and roast our friend.

Let us delight in Walter's stories, memories, and hopes.

Pour forth your mercy and mirth upon us,

And draw us close in the bonds of love,

As we offer our prayers of thanksgiving to You,

In the strong name of our brother Jesus,

Amen.

10

A Toast

Richard Deats

HERE WE CELEBRATE THE LIFE AND WORK OF WALTER WINK AND HIS influence in many areas: biblical scholarship, philosophy, pedagogy, and theology, as well as his work for peace and justice. I am honoring one who has been my best friend since our student days at Southern Methodist University, over fifty years ago.

Many of us have been members of workshops where "Jesus' Third Way" made a lasting impact. After that, we came to understand differently the Sermon on the Mount. This is particularly memorable if Walter ever comes up to you beforehand, and asks if you would mind helping with a role play. You naively agree. Then you're given a swimming suit to wear (under your clothes), and at some key moment during the workshop, you are told to take off everything—except the swim suit. This will dramatize Jesus' teaching about the plight of the accused in court. Personally I've never forgotten that particular role play!

Gandhi maintained that "all miracles are due to the silent and effective working of invisible forces," of which nonviolence is the most invisible and most effective. Walter's focus is on exactly that—what he calls "the redeeming power of the small"—and he has made this come to life in his own biography. Most of us here have read Walter's widely reprinted booklet *Jesus' Third Way*. Not so well known is how that booklet got into South Africa.

Following two visits to South Africa in 1986, Walter wrote *Violence and Nonviolence in South Africa: Jesus' Third Way*, with the subtitle "A Revolutionary New Approach to Theology for a Revolutionary

Situation." It was printed in this country in 1987 but there seemed no way to get it into authoritarian South Africa.

Yet a way was found. A new edition was printed under the simple title, *Jesus' Third Way*, omitting the provocative subtitle. Volunteers from a church in Massachusetts addressed in longhand and on plain wrappers the names and addresses of the 3100 pastors of English-speaking congregations throughout South Africa. The booklets were mailed from different post offices and, as far as I know, most of them reached their destination.

During this same period the Justice and Reconciliation Commission of the South African Council of Churches made possible the funding of a workshop on *Jesus' Third Way*. Walter and I were able to carry this off even though now-notorious Walter was denied a visa. We held the workshop in an out-of-the-way Catholic seminary in the black Republic of Lesotho, free from the visa restrictions in South Africa itself.

Now this was a time of great discouragement. The government had called a state of emergency, and was clamping down on all anti-apartheid activities. Many in those workshops testified that never had the government's efforts been so fierce and restrictive. But then, behold—an old woman from Soweto stood up and testified instead: "The dying horse kicks hardest just before it dies. The government is coming down so hard because it knows it has lost the battle." And she was right! The redeeming power of the small was at work bringing down the mighty South African government.

After the workshop concluded, Walter had to leave Lesotho by a back road through South Africa. Would we be safe? We didn't know. But as he went into the passport office, behold the official was humming "Thine is the Glory, Risen Conquering Lord"—the final hymn we ourselves had sung during the workshop! The official scarcely looked at the passport as he stamped it, thus opening the narrow gate to a visa-less troublemaker.

So it is that Walter's biblical and theological insights have quietly, effectively spread from struggle to struggle, from country to country, assisting in the building of non-violent movements around the world.

It is with immense gratitude that I salute Walter, who has helped awaken the churches from their acceptance of the principalities and powers to a reliance on God who has "chosen things low and contemptible, mere nothings, to overthrow the existing order" (1 Cor 1:28).

11

A Letter

Marcus Borg

DEAR WALTER,

I would love to be with you on this day that celebrates your many years
at Auburn Seminary, traveling the country and the world under their
auspices. And though I wish the best for Auburn, they will have a difficult time finding somebody with your wisdom and your passion and
(is it too much to say?) your charisma.

I know you already know all of what I am about to say about you,
for I have told you all of this in bits and pieces over the years. You know
the high regard and affection I have for you. But *today* is a day for telling
others about how highly and warmly I think of you. So, assuming that
you won't be bored by a litany of accolades, I begin.

Almost two decades before I met you, I knew about you. It was the
fall of 1969. I was in the first year of my doctoral program at Oxford
and had just embarked on three years of reading everything I could
about the historical Jesus. I began with Jesus' relationship with John
the Baptizer, and so I read everything I could find on him, including
especially your 1968 book on John the Baptist.[1] I was impressed. And I
regarded you as the world's leading authority on the subject. Little did
I know that you were only about thirty years old when you wrote the
book, just a few years older than I. But you were a "big name" for me
"way back" in 1969.

That was thirty-six years ago. (Can you believe it?) In the decades
since, my respect and admiration for you and your work has continued

1. Wink, *John the Baptist in the Gospel Tradition*.

to grow. I recommend you and your books to church groups wherever I go (and that's now almost a million miles).

And I also do so in my own books. I especially recommend *Engaging the Powers* and your recent small book for the new Fortress Facet series, *Jesus and Non-Violence*. Indeed, the latter is one of the textbooks in a course on Jesus that I am teaching this term. Students in public universities encounter your thought.

I have learned much from you, as has the discipline of New Testament scholarship as a whole. Several of your themes have become widely shared within the discipline even as they are important to me. Without trying to be comprehensive, I mention the following notions that have now become part of the "accepted wisdom" of many within our academic discipline:

- *The concept and language of "domination systems."* More than anybody else in New Testament studies, you have given us language for the most typical form of political and economic organization in the ancient world, and its importance for understanding Jesus and early Christianity. And you make it clear that domination systems continue in the modern and post-modern world.

- *The claim that Jesus advocated non-violent resistance.* The resistance was both non-violent protest against oppression *and* advocacy of a non-violent strategy for social change. Your exegesis of the sayings in the Sermon on the Mount about loving enemies, turning the other cheek, going the second mile, and giving up your shirt as well as your cloak, are taken seriously by many Jesus scholars. And your presentation of the many times that non-violence has succeeded as a significant means of social change move Jesus' teaching from "unrealistic and naïve" to "practical and wise"—and right.

- *Your work on "the principalities and powers."* This is connected to your emphasis on domination systems, of course. But it deserves separate mention as another distinctive contribution you have made. You have not only highlighted this theme in the New Testament, but you have helped to make us aware that "systemic evil" is bigger than any of us as individuals. Whatever we think ontologically of "the powers," they are real. You, more than any other New Testament scholar of our generation, have helped us to see this.

Well, Walter, I could say more, but I have gone on long enough that perhaps I am boring you. But maybe we don't get bored by praise. So I will say one more thing.

More than any other contemporary biblical scholar that I know of, you have lived out much of what you write about. It's not that the rest of us are hypocrites. But you more than the rest of us have lived your life as a Christian intellectual who moves from thought to *praxis*. You have trained people in many workshops about *praxis*. And you have often engaged in *praxis* yourself, on many occasions—I think especially of your time(s) in South Africa.

Finally, Walter, I will soon be doing what you are doing, retiring from my "institution." It is not a retirement from *vocation*. As you know, there is a beauty to our vocation. So long as we have health and passion, we can keep on keeping on doing what we're doing. We are blessed. Retirement need not mean, "What is my life about *now*?" It can mean, "What am I now free to do?"

And so, on this day that celebrates the contributions that you have made to the world of scholarship *and* the life of the church, I and my beloved Marianne wish you and your beloved June all the best, for all the rest of your life.

With affection and admiration,

Marcus (and Marianne) Borg

12

An Appreciation

Amy-Jill Levine

FOR WALTER WINK, I WOULD GO THE EXTRA MILE, GIVE THE SHIRT off my back, and turn the other cheek. Further, because of Walter—who named, unmasked, and engaged the powers that prompted these expressions in the first place—I am well aware that references to mile, shirt, and cheek are no simple generic descriptors but in fact signal non-violent, proactive responses to systemic evil. Not only has Walter Wink changed the way biblical studies understands Jesus and his cultural context; by doing so he has challenged us all to put into practice what we teach and preach.

We do not always agree. I've fussed at Walter over his early work on the Bible's presentation of sexuality; I fussed over the draft of *The Human Being: Jesus and the Enigma of the Son of the Man*. But in every book I have read by him and in every conversation I have had with him, I have learned something—about history, psychology, medicine, pedagogy, mysticism. The list goes on. And even more that that, Walter is a master, one who models how to converse with another, passionately, without rancor or even defensiveness. Otherwise put, he does more than just study Jesus' "third way." He actually lives it.

To sum up Walter's contributions is impossible. I don't think there *should* be a summation yet, for Walter has much more to teach us. But we can certainly celebrate what he has given us so far. And what better form in which to do so than the *makarism*, the well-known form that starts, "Blessed are"?

Blessed are we who do historical-critical studies of the first century CE, for Walter Wink has shown us how to conjoin rigorous historiography with a profound concern for justice.

Blessed are we who seek "the historical Jesus," for Walter Wink has resurrected the "Son of Man" in a way that would be compelling to anyone, Jew or Greek, female or male.

Blessed are we who seek Shalom between Church and Synagogue, for Walter Wink has demonstrated how Jesus fits within, rather than over and against, his Jewish context, and by doing so has opened another door to Jewish/Christian dialogue.

Blessed are we who seek a place at the table for all, regardless of sexual identity or practice, for Walter Wink has provided the exegetical and hermeneutical grounding by which churches can, with biblical fidelity, welcome all within their doors.

Blessed are we—and blessed especially is Walter—who recognize that the study and practice of religion are not only intellectual but also aesthetic endeavors, how they engage not only intellectual but also aesthetic endeavors, how they engage not only the head and the heart but also the body and the senses. For without June Keener Wink's insistence on embodiment, art, and incarnation, we would all be impoverished.

And blessed are you both, Walter and June, peacemakers, for you truly are children of G-d.

13

An Inspiration

Robert A. Evans

I WANT TO BEGIN BY EXPRESSING THANKS TO AUBURN SEMINARY FOR organizing this event and for giving me the honor of publicly acknowledging our debts to Walter and June Keener Wink for their special partnership as advocates of peace and justice around the world.

My remarks are on behalf of Alice Frazer Evans and myself as the founding directors of Plowshares Institute—a faith-based organization cultivating peace for a more just global community. However, I am confident that these remarks also speak for many of those in the peace movement, which owes Walter a great debt. For Walter Wink has been an intellectual Biblical architect for peace. Along with June, he has been a teacher who embodies transforming and healing methodologies, and he and June are activists who have made peace-building a way of life.

First, let me begin by focusing on Walter's engagement with the principalities and powers in the apartheid regime of South Africa. Desmond Tutu, the current chair of Plowshares Institute International Advisory Council, invited Alice and me to South Africa more than 30 years ago. Our roles as visiting professors and then senior fellows at the Centre for Conflict Resolution at the University of Cape Town and joint programs with South African partner organizations continue to keep us engaged in this remarkable nation. Just as Desmond Tutu's focus has been on the Gospel message of reconciliation, so Walter Wink has been equally committed to the Gospel power of transformation. These concepts of reconciliation and transformation are, of course, intrinsically related, as both Tutu and Wink demonstrate.

One of Walter's most influential and empowering books for peace-builders, *Jesus and Non-Violence: A Third Way*, was shaped by his experiences in South Africa. The Third Way provided an intellectual framework for reflecting and teaching active non-violent resistance to "unmask" the powers of apartheid. Walter's intellectual reflection and his teaching methodologies influenced incalculable numbers of people in the struggle, ranging from the South African Council of Churches and Gun-Free South Africa to Dutch Reformed pastors. In the 1980s, Walter's commitment to be a companion in the process of reconciliation and transformation in South Africa was so strong that when he was denied a visa, he managed to enter South Africa illegally, through the Lesotho border. At this time, we knew many religious leaders trying to sneak out of South Africa, but not very many who were seeking to sneak in!

Walter did this in order to join South African colleagues in teaching non-violent resistance. Following his leadership role in these workshops, Walter joined a Plowshares Institute traveling seminar that was seeking to inform North American civic and religious leaders about the realities of South African apartheid and the heretical theology that shaped these government policies. Over the years Plowshares traveling seminars informed and motivated numerous preachers and theologians, including Rev. Jim Forbes from Riverside Church and Prof. Delores Williams from Union Theological Seminary.

Walter was not only shaped by his experience in South Africa, he also made significant contributions to its liberation and transformation to a non-racial, democratic, non-sexist, more just society. Alice and I had the privilege in February of participating in an artistic celebration and conference to mark the tenth anniversary of the Truth and Reconciliation Commission at the University of Pretoria. Patron and keynote speaker for the event was Archbishop Emeritus Desmond Tutu, the chair of the Truth and Reconciliation Commission. Walter's contributions were publicly acknowledged during more than one of these conference events.

Wink's trilogy on the powers has both informed and guided peace and justice advocates in our own attempts to name, unmask and engage the powers of domination and to grapple with the myth of redemptive violence. These struggles are clearly demonstrated in polarized global and national debates about the doctrines of peaceful, active non-violent resistance and pre-emptive military action. Walter's study of the principalities and powers has assisted peace and justice advocates in both their analysis of and their challenges to this state philosophy of domination.

One of Plowshares' experiences with Walter's insights was in a three-year program in Los Angeles and Philadelphia titled "Christians Empowering for Reconciliation with Justice." One of the assigned texts for participants was the manuscript for the then unpublished Powers that Be, Walter's integration of central insights from the Powers trilogy. In a diverse group of participants from a variety of theological traditions, some thought that this was the most important interpretation of the Bible they had ever encountered. (Others thought it was the height of heresy.) It is clear that Walter's challenging scholarship evokes extreme responses as people are challenged by this intellectual Biblical architect to think in new ways about the Bible.

Secondly, Walter is a teacher who, accompanied by June, embodies transforming and healing methodologies. If you have been in one of Walter and June's workshops, you have experienced their ability to integrate body, mind, and spirit. Their creative engagement with prayer, application, exercises and movement have led innumerable people into a transforming experience with the biblical text. In the late 1970s, Walter introduced me to what I came to call "communal exegesis." We were colleagues on the faculty of Hartford Seminary developing a new program to equip pastors and lay leaders for transforming roles within the church. Walter's approach to engaging the Biblical text moved me to question not only my theology, but my life. The entire faculty of Hartford Seminary used to gather on Monday morning under Walter's leadership for Bible study. Having taught in a number of seminaries in the U.S. and around the world, this was my only experience of an entire faculty gathered together on a regular basis for an encounter with the sacred text in order to be informed and empowered by common study. It was a process of engagement that I both loved and hated. This methodology of encountering the text informed, challenged, and sometimes disconcerted the participants.

Alice and I have adapted this method of Bible study for programs that have included civic organizations, congregations, and many theological seminaries in the United States and abroad. We employ Walter's approach to encounter—and be encountered by—the Hebrew scriptures, New Testament parables, the Qur'an and even the Preamble to the South African Constitution, which is seen as a sacred text in many nations of Africa.

Walter's approach to transforming Bible study has also been incorporated in a Plowshares pedagogy born in South Africa titled Peace Skills for Community Mediators.[1] It has challenged government representatives, religious leaders and the civic activists in workshops for potential peace builders on five continents. Alice and I have just returned from Indonesia, which has both the largest Muslim and Reformed Christian populations in the world. Plowshares' joint project with the Indonesian Ministry of Law and Human Rights is designed to equip government leaders, law enforcement officers, university professors and human rights NGOs to integrate human rights, democracy and conflict transformation. Walter's interactive pedagogy is firmly planted in a curriculum that seeks to equip national leaders for the significant transition this society is experiencing. This past July the people of Indonesia experienced their first direct election of the president, vice president and members of Parliament, with 80% of the registered voters participating. All of the international observers confirmed this was a free and fair election. Following the election, the Minister of Justice reflected that perhaps some time in the future the United States might follow the Indonesian democratic example of direct election for their president and vice president.

Plowshares Institute, also in conjunction with the Ministry of Law and Human Rights, is launching a new project for the tsunami-devastated province of Aceh in the northern tip of the island of Sumatra. This small province was facing the devastating death of 185,000 people, and an additional 500,000 left homeless. Estimates indicate that one-third of all families in the United States contributed to the relief and reconstruction of areas affected by the tsunami, including much of Indonesia. In Aceh province, a formerly suspicious Muslim majority greeted U.S. military forces leading humanitarian recovery and restoration efforts with appreciation. This kind of response is reflected in Walter's advocacy of using the power of military forces for peace and justice when the focus is on healing and renewal.

1. Kraybill, Frazer Evans, and Evans, *Peace Skills*; see also Frazer Evans and Evans, *Peace Skills: Leaders Guide*.

Plowshares' seminars for Acehnese civic and religious leaders will focus on both conflict transformation and trauma healing. The sessions will include the study of texts from the Bible and Qu'ran following Walter's open questions, which have already been translated into bahasa Indonesia, the nation's official language. Plowshares endorses a premise akin to the one that undergirds Walter's international commitments to peace and justice—the crucial idea that both relief and reconstruction are threatened without attention to reconciliation.

Walter's focus on transformation is central to his work as both an intellectual architect and a transforming teacher. His contributions to the Peace Skills manual and leader's guide have been disseminated not only in English and Indonesian but also in Spanish, as well as portions in Afrikaans, Korean, and Chinese. His work as a scholar and a teacher truly has had an international impact.

And thirdly, Walter and June have been activists who have made peace-building a way of life. They have integrated their commitments and beliefs into a healing and transforming lifestyle. Walter is not only engaged in writing, teaching, and preaching; he is also practicing his own message in New York and Washington and Sandisfield, Massachusetts. Walter and June witness to their commitments for peace and justice in their open opposition to the war in Iraq and nuclear proliferation, as well as in their advocacy for a wild and scenic Farmington River as an expression of deep concern for the environment.

Walter is a consistent activist in his life in the church, in society, and in the world. He provokes students in the classroom, congregations, and secular audiences through his distinctive form of Socratic dialogue. However, Walter has a gentle and informing style that is seductively attractive even to those who oppose some of his insights about the biblical text. I recall an occasion when Alice and I invited Walter to come to the Presbytery of Southern New England to engage the clergy and lay members in a dialogue about ordination of gays and lesbians. His approach to the biblical text was so persuasive and startlingly alarming that many in that audience came to see the issue of the leadership of gays and lesbians in the life of the church as a fundamental issue of liberation. I should also add that some were so alarmed by the persuasiveness of this encounter that they are reluctant to speak to Alice and me to this day. So being one of Walter's "soul mates" can also be dangerous, just as an encounter with the biblical text in new ways can make one both more vulnerable and more open to transformation.

In closing, I want to reaffirm for Alice and me, along with scores of other advocates for peace and justice around the world, that Walter is indeed an intellectual architect, a passionate and compassionate teacher, and an unrelenting activist. We are grateful to have Walter and June as companions on the way and as friends. Thank you both.

14

A Partnership

Tansy Chapman

I was asked to speak on the subject of "Integration and Embodiment," both of which are epitomized in the work of June Keener Wink. Rather than using words for something that is ultimately experiential, I wish that we could push back the chairs and tables and that June could lead us in movement.

There have been a succession of serious talks and reflections on Walter's work today, and many thoughts and ideas have been stirred up in us, but how do we integrate these ideas so that they become an essential part of who we are?

Well, before June joined Walter fully in the workshops, Walter had this very much in mind. He did not want the results of his lectures and Bible study groups to remain in the classroom. From the start, Walter was concerned about how to help people find integration between body, mind and spirit. He used numerous creative rituals and worked with art. It was not until June began working with Walter, however, that they were able to build into their workshops a major component of movement and art. What June brings to the workshops is a vivacious sense of integrity, an ever deeper commitment, and a boundless creativity in the application of the texts they work on.

It was Walter Wink's small book *Transforming Bible Study* that led me to the Winks over twenty years ago at a workshop at Trinity Episcopal Church in Topsfield, Massachusetts. I knew that Walter had already begun to introduce art, clay and drama to his workshops, but I had not anticipated being led in movement by June Keener Wink, or the impact their combined work would have, and continues to have, on my own healing and faith development.

For those who have been led by June in dance and movement, either in partnership with Walter or in her solo workshops, and who have been drawn into Scripture passages through an integrative process, you will have your own memories of what it is like to be part of these workshops. You will know what a transformative experience it can be to dance with June.

Who is this June Keener Wink? What is it that she does that is so clearly innovative? What has she developed over the years that we can recognize and describe—which is built on, but takes us further than, what has been done before? What makes her work so boundlessly creative and unique? Why can we call her a pioneer in this field?

How did she start? June tells the story of being "almost middle aged" and feeling herself caught in the expectations of her role as a woman in the culture in which she lived. (However, June's vitality and youthful appearance makes me doubt whether she has ever yet reached middle age!) As one way of finding freedom and self-expression, she began to work with clay and has become an expert and creative potter. On one of her large pots she has painted different pictures of her spiritual development, including a picture of herself perfectly dressed in high heels, hat and gloves, arms crossed tightly across her chest, obviously inhibited. The figure next to it is of a woman dancing freely so that the spirit of God within her was opening her up to the possibility of becoming a whole human being. On the same pot she has painted the Spirit with wings.

She is an example to all of us of what it means to be fully embodied. Her faith is incarnational. No longer is she caught up in the conventional cultural construction of the body in our society. She is supple and free to move as Wisdom herself directs her.

First of all, June creates a calm space for us to enter into with silence. She invites us to remove our shoes. In the middle of the room she places one of her dancing flame lamps. The flame dances as a symbol of God's dancing and moving spirit in our midst and in the world. Soft music is playing.

June invites us to begin to stretch our bodies. As she does so she lets us know that all of us are welcome, whatever our physical ability or emotional state. We are included just as we are. (This is a time when we may feel great resistance and anxiety, and June is aware of this.) Her words are comforting and reassuring and deeply rooted in the Judeo-Christian faith.

June reminds us that we are grounded in the earth, to start to breathe deeply, that God is breathing through us, and that we are held in the arms of God. She speaks of the Hebrew word *Nephesh*, which means heart, body and soul as one. As Christians, she says, our tradition has often taught us to deny, or to brutalize, or to repress, the body, which splits the body from soul. This attitude is called dualism—and it is one of the most profound and damaging splits in Western Civilization. In movement we are engaged with the whole self, for as we start moving our bodies, that very movement uses every part of us: our minds, our feelings and our bodies. June is aware that many of the participants, particularly in healing workshops, have a history of trauma and disconnection with their physical bodies.

And then, as we begin to move, we are reminded that we are already part of the dance, that the creative One is dancing in and through us. We are encouraged to keep our eyes lowered so as not to watch others. The movement is not about performance, but rather encourages spontaneity and freedom from the bonds of self-consciousness. June also helps us to accept our own bodies, and to recognize how in so many ways we regard our bodyselves with distrust and even absolute dislike, rather than celebrating the beauty and gift of our unique physicality. The body, June reminds us, is the temple of the Holy Spirit.

The movement may begin in a number of ways, depending on June's boundless creativity. For example, in order to introduce a framework for moving she may gently encourage us to explore our own kinesphere (the personal space around each of us) by simply painting imaginary planes, which she has us enlarge as we move around the room. It is only later that we may realize with respect and awareness that the space around each person, whoever they are, is holy. She may have us move and dance, leading with an arm, an elbow, a knee, a hip, and suddenly we are spinning around the room. . . . Energy is released, freeing us from inhibitions that have kept us bound up. Another time, she may invite us to move with another person in harmony and then move on, with each creating our own individual dance in relation to a partner and eventually end up in larger groups. We begin to form a community, which gives depth to the total workshop.

June may have us imagine ourselves as some object, and have us dance the movement that, we discover, is intrinsic in all matter. This again may be done with one or several other people. She also invites us to find something in nature (i.e., a rock, a leaf, a flower or branch) and to examine it in great detail, and then to dance the qualities of the piece of nature that has chosen us. The movement reminds us of our connectedness with all things created in our world. There is great variety in the way June leads us, but whatever she introduces, one realizes that it has been carefully thought out and reflects the cumulative knowledge gained from hundreds of workshop with many different people all over the world. For instance, while in South Africa, she specifically worked with nonviolent experiences in movement with all faiths at all economic levels.

What has happened to us at the end of one of the Winks' workshops? And what has June's part done to contribute to the way we live our lives as more-fully-human beings? For each person the answer is different. In my own experience, I have realized that although June rarely makes an explicit verbal connection with a text Walter has been talking about, in the course of the days dancing with her, we realize that what we have read, discussed, and pondered has become incarnate. The spirit of God is moving in a new way. What has bound us up has been released. If we are not aware of our bodies, how can we possibly have empathy for the lives of other people? If we are isolated, how can we ever form community? If we despise our own bodies, how can we ever know intimacy with other human beings?

June is immensely gifted. Her work needs to be taught to others. We need to learn from her courage and introduce movement into our own varied ministries. June has demonstrated that the work she has developed can be taken all over the world and to many different cultures. She is a bearer of grace and healing.

How does this relate to justice or societal changes? Here are her own words: "We strive for spontaneity in our bodies. Spontaneity is the ability to respond to what God calls us to do. For me it has been to hold the body of a dirty, tired child in the slums of Rio and to feel the pain of living in that little six year old who was trying to get a little money by shining shoes all day. To me it is visiting the townships in South Africa, entering their tiny tin houses and smelling with them the stench of sewage that runs by their door. It's being able to bend, to stretch and twist with God. I believe that Jesus had soft knees. He could move in any direction God wanted. He went where he was called. We too need those soft knees in order to be effective in this world."

15

A Testament

Balfour Brickner

I THANK YOU FOR LETTING ME BE A PART OF THIS CELEBRATION. AFTER listening to the other presentations here, I have the feeling I went to the wrong seminary. And I'll tell you something: the people who ran that seminary were absolutely *convinced* I was in the wrong one! We didn't have charismatic preachers who were activists. We had a different variety.

I've been asked to offer reflections about "Walter's Homosexuality." Seriousness aside for a moment, let me say that I'm not really comfortable putting it quite that way. Instead, I will address myself to his writings on the subject. The rest I leave to someone who knows him a little better!

As you can tell, I wish this were a roast. Because Walter Wink, if anything else, is eminently roastable. And you know why? Because first of all, he knows what and who he is. He has an enormous sense of self. And secondly, he has a quixotic sense of humor. You don't always see it coming. All of a sudden it's in your face, and you find yourself laughing like hell. You can roast someone like that.

But I will settle instead for this moment of coronation. One miraculous book Walter, and sainthood will be yours. Protestant sainthood, that is. It's a strange variety, which we don't have in our tradition.

But enough of that. I came not to bury Caesar, but to praise him. Walter is also wonderfully praisable.

Now like many of us here, I am absolutely addicted to speaking and to writing. I am actually at work on a new manuscript, a defense of our new attitudes towards human sexuality. One of the chapters is a chapter on "Homosexuality: Our Changing Views," with a subheading called "Homosexuality and the Bible." This is a realm I enter reluctantly—first because this voluminous matter has already been dealt with elsewhere. Books and pamphlets are readily available for anyone wishing to know what the Bible says about homosexuality. And one of the best and most concise treatments of this topic appeared in a succinct pamphlet entitled, also, "Homosexuality and the Bible," written by my dear friend and colleague Walter Wink. I rely on him to lead me through the New Testament references, an area in which I have little expertise. However, it seems to me that both of our traditions—Judaism and Christianity—seem to agree that homosexuality, while biblically "condemned," must also been seen in the context of the sex ethic of the day.

As Walter points out, "there is no Biblical sex ethic. Instead, [the Bible] exhibits a variety of sexual mores, some of which changed over the thousand-year span of biblical history. Mores are unreflective customs accepted by a given community. . . . The Bible knows only a *love ethic* . . . . Sexuality cannot be separated off from the rest of life. No sex act is 'ethical' in and of itself, without reference to the rest of a person's life, the pattern of the culture, the special circumstances faced, and the will of God."[1]

I would love to have been able to write that. I am delighted instead to quote it. That quotation draws from Walter's wondrous pamphlet. It is a masterpiece of information and wit, and it is not above poking a few holes into our pious hypocrisy. Let me share more of its insights with you.

> The law of Moses allowed for divorce (Deut. 24: 1-4); Jesus categorically forbids it (Mark 10: 1-12; Matt. 19.9 softens his severity). Yet many Christians, in clear violation of a command of Jesus, have been divorced. Why, then, do some of these very people consider themselves eligible for baptism, church membership, communion, and ordination, but not homosexuals? What makes the one so much greater a sin than the other, especially considering the fact that Jesus never even mentioned homosexuality, but explicitly condemned divorce? Yet we ordain divorcees. Why not homosexuals?[2]

And again:

1. Wink, "Homosexuality and the Bible," 10–11.
2. Ibid., 7.

In addition, when a man acted like a woman sexually, male dignity was compromised. It was a degradation, not only in regard to himself, but for every other male. And the repugnance felt toward homosexuality was not just that it was deemed unnatural, but also that it was considered alien behavior, representing yet one more incursion of pagan civilization into Jewish life. On top of that is the more universal repugnance heterosexuals tend to feel for acts and orientations foreign to them. (Left-handedness has evoked something of the same response in many cultures.)[3]

While Walter is good at describing the attitudes toward homosexuality in the Hebrew texts, he is at the top of his game when it comes to describing this in the New Testament. He writes:

> For Christians, Old Testament texts have to be weighed against the New. Consequently, Paul's unambiguous condemnation of homosexual behavior in Rom 1:26–27 must be the centerpiece of any discussion.
>
> > For this reason God gave them up to degrading passions. Their women exchanged natural intercourse for unnatural, and in the same way also the men, giving up natural intercourse with women, were consumed with passion for one another. Men committed shameless acts with men and received in their own persons the due penalty for their error.
>
> No doubt Paul was unaware of the distinction between sexual orientation, over which one has apparently very little choice, and sexual behavior, over which one does. He seemed to assume that those whom he condemned were heterosexuals who were acting contrary to nature, "leaving," "giving up," or "exchanging" their regular sexual orientation for that which was foreign to them. Paul knew nothing of the modern psychosexual understanding of homosexuals as persons whose orientation is fixed early in life, or perhaps even genetically in some cases. For such persons, having heterosexual relations would be acting contrary to nature, "leaving," "giving up" or "exchanging" their natural sexual orientation for one that was unnatural to them.
>
> > In other words, Paul really thought that those whose behavior he condemned were "straight," and that they were behaving in ways that were unnatural to them. Paul believed that everyone was "straight." He had no concept of homosexual orientation.

3. Ibid., 2.

> The idea was not available in his world. There are people that
> are genuinely homosexual by nature (whether genetically or as
> a result of upbringing no one really knows, and it is irrelevant).
> For such a person it would be acting contrary to nature to have
> sexual relations with a person of the opposite sex.[4]

I wish I could read this entire pamphlet to you; obviously I cannot.
What I can tell you is that the acceptance of homosexuality in contemporary society is well under way, and even those who hate gays know it.
It will happen, whether religious bodies help or hinder the process. And
unfortunately there are more religious bodies in the process of hindering
it than there are trying to help it. Religious groups need to realize that
by obtuseness, denial, or open hostility, they can only delay the process;
they cannot reverse it.

Consider for a moment the benefits to be enjoyed by all of society
if we encouraged, of loving and committed homosexuals, exactly what
we expect from heterosexual—the fostering of mutual affection, care
and support, the intensification of our capacity to endure pain and tragedy through sharing, the overcoming of loneliness, even the nurturing
of home life for children.

Homosexuality is neither contagious nor infectious. It cannot be
transferred by a teacher, or by a clergy person who leads her congregation in prayer. What is infectious, however, is fear—fear of contact, fear
of friendship, fear of people who are (for whatever reason) "different."
And what are contagious are ridicule and prejudicial acts against them.
These breed contempt, scorn, and derision, and these are highly dangerous social diseases. Walter Wink is courageous enough and wise enough
to have brought these truths into open light, and in open confrontation even with members of his own community who do not share his
enlightened views. Yet they will, and in a decade they'll wonder what
took them so long.

As Jew, I know well the evils of such behavior, and what cruelty
such thinking can unleash. I have been its victim. We all have. And
we have a responsibility, within our lifetime, to bring a little closer to
humankind the teachings of Walter Wink on homosexuality and the
Bible.

4. Ibid., 3.

16

A Recollection

Bonnie Rosborough

WALTER, I HAVE BEEN ASKED TO SPEAK ABOUT THE IMPACT OF YOUR work on the practice of parish ministry. I really can only speak about your impact on me, a practitioner of ministry; and I want to do that, briefly, from two angles.

First, I must acknowledge how threatening you were to me when I arrived at Union in 1973 as a very young and unformed Master of Divinity student. Your revolutionary book, *The Bible and Human Transformation*, had been published just before I arrived; and it raised quite a dust storm up at the seminary. Most of those issues eluded me, but what was unmistakable to my eye was the fact that something in you had taken hold and would not let go. There was something you were so excited about, so driven by, so dedicated to that you were willing to give your life and career to it. That was impressive, very impressive, but while it excited me, I must confess that it also frightened me.

For you were a man possessed. (I now know that the better word is "charismatic.") The gifts resident in you are, indeed, powerful, the stuff of life and death. You taught me, by modeling it, that God's gifts to us are both precious and demanding, and to be faithful to them is a life long, oft times sacrificial task.

The second thing that I learned from you is that the Word of God is alive, sharper than a two edged sword, cutting both ways (to borrow from Hebrews). I suppose that, as a Christian, I should have known this long before coming to Seminary—and certainly before venturing to serve the church. But, somehow, I didn't, until, with your shepherding, the Word came alive in my life and study. That Living Word, indeed, has transformed me as well as nourished and inspired all my ministry—preaching, teaching and pastoral care.

Would I have been so blessed without your tutelage? I would hope so, for it is unimaginable to me how I might serve the church without the Word's vitality and grace. But I thank and praise God that it was by your charisms that I came to better understand God's address. Thank you.

17

Envoi

Barbara G. Wheeler

ABOVE AND BEYOND. WALTER, YOUR HISTORY IS ONE OF EXPECTATIONS exceeded. You chose to do your life's work in one of the most traditional of academic fields. The topics and methods of Biblical research are well-marked paths, the teaching approaches long-established and standardized. At the start of your career at Union you broke both molds, pioneering a new, highly controversial Bible study method with an ambitious goal—human transformation. At the same time, you brought unorthodox ideas, from psychology and other fields, to your teaching and research.

You came to Auburn almost three decades ago with a one-item job description—to teach your innovative approach to Bible study as widely across the church as possible. On your own initiative, you expanded the assignment. You integrated June Keener Wink's creative work with your own, creating a dynamic teaching team. And on your own time you became a highly productive scholar, turning out far more published work than most academics whose advancement depends on research: innumerable reviews, essays, pamphlets, chapters, books—a whole trilogy! In these numerous publications you advanced a series of ideas about scripture and human life which have shaped the work of many other scholars and which even those who disagreed with you most strenuously have had to think and talk about. Above and beyond, indeed.

Finally, and most exceptionally, Walter, you—unlike many professors—have made your mark in the world, as much as in the classroom and the library. You haven't just written about the principalities and powers; you have engaged them, in all the arenas that this volume lifts up and celebrates. In so doing, you have advanced important movements and causes, but you've also accomplished something more: you have convinced lots of people, outside the church as well as in it, that the Bible is a means of power, the power with which God graces all of us to love and heal the world. As a result, you—probably more than anyone of your generation—have created interest in, respect for, even love of Biblical studies beyond the walls of academe.

I have no doubt that in so-called retirement you will continue to exceed expectations. All of us at Auburn send you to the next stage with gratitude, for you have so greatly enhanced Auburn's reputation for powerful education and original ideas. You have our affection and our highest admiration.

18

Final Toast

Robert Raines

MY WIFE CINDY AND I WENT TO KIRKRIDGE IN THE FALL OF 1974, and soon heard about an exciting Bible teacher at Union Seminary, someone called Walter Wink. A few months later we got permission to attend one of Walter's classes. He used the Socratic method, which got students so interactively engaged that the energy in the room was really soaring. Lots of learning, we thought—very powerful. We must get this guy to Kirkridge! So I read Walter's book on *The Bible in Human Transformation*, and invited him to Kirkridge in the fall of 1976. Thus began a love affair between Kirkridge and Walter. He visited four times a year in the early years, for five-day events. He has been there more than forty times in thirty years. We watched people struggle and search. We watched them gain insight and create community. We watched them *experience* transformation. For Walter was following in the steps of Paul, who certainly did not say "Be informed by the renewal of your mind." He said, "Be transformed . . ." *Walter is an agent of that transformation.*

Sometimes he would come to Kirkridge fearing that a mysterious illness had attacked him, and occasionally he was actually right about that. His physical and psychic vulnerabilities opened his heart to other people's sufferings and made him humanly accessible to his students. He could send the gospel material deep into their hearts and lives. Then, in the mid-1980s, June began to assist him with body movement meditation, and before long June was Walter's full partner in the workshops, enriching the experience for others and, in the meantime, keeping Walter happy—which was no small benefit. *For Walter is a wounded healer.*

Did you know that Walter has beautiful feet? You may not have noticed this, though his feet are certainly large enough. But all you need to do is remember: "How beautiful upon the mountains are the feet of the messenger of peace." Walter has been announcing peace in word and deed across this country and abroad, all throughout his ministry. In 1982, at the height of the Cold War, some Kirkridge folk went to the great Central Park rally and protest. We have a marvelous photo of Walter, June, Rebecca and other friends, standing near the Kirkridge banner. Unlike some preachers and teachers, Walter took risks for the gospel: he would put his body where his mouth was; he walked the walk as well as talking the talk. That kind of integrity deepened his authority, and took him out on the streets, where, of course, Jesus performed much of his ministry. *Walter is a peacemaker.*

I have long thought that how we pray reveals more of our real theology than anything else. I have heard Walter pray from the heart. He was never embarrassed to ask for our prayers. I, too, love his phrase: "History belongs to the intercessors, who believe the future into being." Once I asked Walter: "Do you believe in eternal life?" He replied: "If God who dreamed up Creation couldn't figure out something marvelous beyond death, I'd be disappointed in God." *Walter, you see, is a believer.*

So, Walter: Cindy and I salute you—transformer, healer, peacemaker, believer, and through it all, our dear friend. We love you, and commend to you Wendell Berry's agenda for the rest of your life. So, friend,

> . . . every day do something
> that won't compute. Love the Lord.
> Love the world. Work for nothing. . . .
> Love someone who does not deserve it.
> Denounce the government and embrace
> the flag . . .
> Ask the questions that have no answers.
> . . . Plant sequoias.
> . . . Laugh.
> . . . Be joyful
> though you have considered all the facts. . . .
> Practice resurrection.[1]

1. Berry, "Manifesto."

PART THREE

Enigmas *of the* Future

19

A New Spirituality and Hope for the Future

Some Contributions from
the Scholarship of Walter Wink

Joseph C. Hough, Jr.

MORE THAN ANYTHING ELSE, MY DEBT TO WALTER WINK HAS BEEN his profound challenge to me not only to live from and in the teachings of Jesus, but to recognize afresh that it is possible for Jesus as the "Human One" to live in me. By a circuitous route, the "cosmic and mythical Jesus" of my childhood might become a deep living presence that actually comes alive in me. I shall say more about that later, but first some history.

I have never claimed to be a scholar of the New Testament, but for most of my life I have tried very hard to live from the accounts of Jesus conveyed to me by the reading of the Bible, a regular practice in my home. I have had less success than many in this effort, but that relative failure has little to do with the intention and effort I have brought to the figure of Jesus. Over time, his importance for me has waxed and waned, as the necessary and liberating deconstruction of my early literalist understanding occurred during my studies of the New Testament.

It was Rudolf Bultmann who for a time was my guide in the ongoing internal dialogue with the Jesus of the New Testament. In 1921, Bultmann published his important book, *The History of the Synoptic Tradition*, in which he argued that virtually nothing could be known about the Jesus of History.[1] Discounting any attempts to draw a picture of the historical Jesus, including that of Albert Schweitzer, who pictured Jesus as a failed apocalyptic prophet having little relevance for modern

1. Bultmann, *History of the Synoptic Tradition.*

times, Bultmann declared that the historical Jesus was not accessible to us. What we have before us in the New Testament, he said, was an interpretation of a shadowy figure created by the faith of the Church. In spite of sporadic attempts by James Robinson and others to revive interest in the historical Jesus, Bultmann's view dominated New Testament scholarship, and my own understanding, until recent times. Recently, however, all this has changed.

Prompted by discoveries and translations of a host of new manuscripts, including the Dead Sea Scrolls and the Nag Hammadi Library (discovered in 1947 and 1945, respectively), scholars have access to a vastly expanded knowledge of the intellectual context of New Testament times and the wide diversity of teachings about Jesus that existed soon after his death. In addition, advances in cultural anthropology have enabled us to get a much better picture of the cultural setting in which Jesus taught, bringing greater clarity to his teachings than ever before. Finally, new studies of Roman and Jewish historical sources have presented us with the possibility of revolutionary understandings of the accounts of the crucifixion and resurrection of Jesus.

Since 1980, more than 50 books have been written dealing with the historical Jesus, more than in all the previous history of New Testament scholarship. Concentrated among a group of scholars known as *The Jesus Seminar*, this new scholarship has changed the shape of New Testament studies. For me, the impact of writings such as Marcus Borg's book, *Meeting Jesus Again for the First Time* and John Dominic Crossan's book, *Jesus: a Revolutionary Biography,* have been especially important.

The Jesus who appears to us through this new scholarship is a very different Jesus from the one most of us have been accustomed to imagining. He is no longer a messianic figure cast in previous interpretations of the title "Son of Man," nor is he a Davidic figure come to restore Jerusalem and the surrounding promised land to Israel's rule. This Jesus does not claim to be the divine judge or the cosmic principle of truth. He is not consumed by hope for the end times or the physical reconstruction of the world, nor does he make any claims for himself to be divine or even superhuman. The one we encounter is a Jewish peasant or artisan whose ministry was largely confined to Galilee until his single pilgrimage took him to Jerusalem for the fateful last days of his life. And in his home country, about 95 percent of the people were poor, and the remaining 5 percent lived rather well. The contrast between the rich and poor was very stark. Jesus, the child of a carpenter, was among the poor and related to them directly.

He began his teaching career rather late in life. The average age of death for males in his class and time was about 29, and that was about the age at which he began his public teaching. Nearly all his ministry was carried out in Galilee, and he often taught small groups in homes. Most of his teachings that have been passed on to us are in the form of parables and aphorisms.

Jesus was fully and thoroughly Jewish. By the age of eleven, he was immersed in the teachings of the *Tanakh*. He was often in the synagogue, and though he appropriated the rhetorical forms of the Greeks familiar to him from the surrounding Greek culture of his homeland, his teaching was always directed to the Jewish people he knew. He had a vision of God as the one who loved the poor and had special compassion on them. Therefore, Jesus' sayings reflected his deep compassion for the poor people to whom he often spoke: "Blessed are you poor, for yours is the kingdom of heaven." "Foxes have dens and birds of the air have nests, but you sons of Adam have no place to lay your heads." "The spirit of the Lord is upon me because he has anointed me to preach good news to the poor." His compassion for the poor aroused in him a righteous indignation that was reflected in his practice. In short, Jesus' teaching was highly subversive. His life and teaching were in direct conflict with custom. He cared neither for social conventions nor religious rules that separate human beings into classes of social or economic privilege or religious superiority. He ate and socialized with prostitutes and with tax collectors.

The kingdom of God he envisioned was not of another world, nor was it a royal restoration of David's political kingdom in this world. It was not even an earthly kingdom ruled by a heavenly ruler who would destroy the earth and create it again. The kingdom of God in Jesus' teaching was about the vision of what the world could be like if, under the rule of God, everyone is loved. It was a kingdom from which no one was an outcast. The sick, the demented, the prostitutes, the tax collectors, all of them would come to the table, and all would dine together, with the spirit of God hosting the great community of compassion. In light of this, it is highly possible that the Epistle of James, attributed to Jesus' brother, the bishop of the church in Jerusalem, is closer to his teachings than are, generally, Paul's letters.

One can only imagine the profound change in our religious practice if we took this picture of Jesus seriously. Our Eucharist might be seen as a universal meal to which all of God's people have an open invitation. It would no longer be a symbol of exclusion as it often is now and has been in the past. On the contrary, it would become the symbol of inclusion. In this meal there would be no marginalized people. All who wished to eat could come to the table.

Our baptism would be our pledge to care for each other and our world, not a separation of the saved and pure from the unsaved and impure. If beliefs seemed to hurt others, we could change them to reflect our vision of a compassionate God who is with us all. Our ministries would most often move among the poorest and the neediest. Our spirituality would become as natural as breathing, and our worship would focus on praise to a compassionate and merciful God in our world here and now.

Walter Wink has been very much involved in shaping this exciting new scholarship and, more broadly, spirituality and religious practice. As Bruce Chilton points out,[2] Wink has been critical of the work of much contemporary New Testament scholarship on particular grounds: namely, that the method and approach has been characterized by a pervasive positivism and objectivism, a failing that has resulted in the omission of what Wink describes as the spiritual dimension of the New Testament witness.

Just what is meant by this broad ranging critique became clearer to me when I read his 2002 book, *The Human Being: Jesus and the Enigma of the Son of the Man.* Relying heavily on a Jungian construct of archetypes that he brings to his interpretation of Jesus, Wink transforms the revolutionary prophet, the Jewish apocalyptic, into The Son of Man, the one prophesied and foretold by Ezekiel and Daniel. He was surely *not* the Son of Man who was to be the literal ruler of the world, the lord of all kingdoms. But the impact he had upon his disciples, particularly their transformation after the crucifixion and resurrection experiences, indicate, for Wink, that something real, something "objective" happened that led them to experience Jesus as alive "in them." This, says Wink, was the realization that they had experienced something radically new in the humanity of Jesus and that simultaneously something

2. See Chilton's remarks in this volume.

happened to the very image of God. The disciples had seen Jesus do all kinds of miraculous things such as healing the sick and casting out demons. After Pentecost, they recognized that those same powers had been transferred to them. The spirit that worked through Jesus now was working in them.

For the disciples, Jesus at his ascension entered into the "archetypical realm." Not only did Jesus create the archetype of the truly human (Son of Man), but "the very image of God was altered by the sheer force of Jesus' being. God would never be the same. Jesus had indelibly imprinted the divine. God had everlastingly entered the human." In other words, the ascension signifies that something had altered the consciousness of the disciples themselves. "They would never again be able to think of God apart from Jesus."[3] God has become incarnate in Jesus and Jesus is now inseparably joined with our knowledge of and experience of God.

This short summary of a very complex argument certainly does not do justice to Wink's proposal, but it is sufficient to indicate that here the search for the historical Jesus has moved beyond the description of the life, the times, and the teachings of Jesus. What Wink is suggesting is that one cannot understand the historical impact of Jesus on human beings then and now apart from some conception of the powerful spiritual force he brings that alters our vision of who we are and what we can be. Whether or not one can assent to the Jungian constructs in which Wink's argument is cast, he has, in my view, opened the door to new possibilities for a Christian mysticism that could connect to the growing interest in spirituality manifested in a generation of seekers probing for something more than sagacious teaching and moral exhortation.

I am also convinced that Wink's understanding of Jesus' humanity might enable a more profound openness to the spiritual insights of other religious traditions. If, in his words, the true archetype of The Human Being is the spirit of compassion who resists the domination of the powers of the earth, perhaps we can arrive at a point where Christians recognize our common Human Being in representatives of other traditions who have discovered that the true spirit of humanity is the spirit of compassion that cares for the poor and resists all injustice and domination. That discovery would open the way for more creative expressions

3. Wink, *The Human Being*, 152.

of Christian affirmations of the centrality of Jesus for our faith. It would also allow us to recognize the transformative power of other religious traditions that are evident in faithful practitioners of those traditions. This would not, of course, mean that all religions are the same. Since religions are expressions of culture, it should be expected that their perceptions of spirituality will take different forms. Yet, the affirmation that Jesus is archetypically The Human Being could broaden the possibility that we shall be open to a revolutionary "shock of recognition" that will yield between several great religious traditions new possibilities for mutual respect and joint efforts for world transformation. Jesus' words in Luke 9:50 ring loudly, and pregnantly.

In addition, I have great appreciation for Wink's careful attention to the apocalyptic aspects of Jesus' teaching. He, like so many New Testament scholars today, dismisses any notion that the teaching of Jesus was focused upon some cataclysmic history-ending time of judgment and destruction. He even doubts that Mark 13, a concentrated depository of apocalyptic thinking, was authored by Jesus. Nor does he believe that the violent portrayal of the last judgment in the book of Revelation is in accord with Jesus' teaching.

Of course, fascination with predicting the End Times began long before John wrote the Book of Revelation. It is rooted in the Jewish tradition as early as the exile of the Jewish people to Babylon 587 years before the Common Era. The book of Ezekiel, written in the context of the exile, is the best example of the ancient yearning for divine intervention to punish the wicked and oppressive enemies and to restore the land of Israel to the Jewish people. John, a Jewish-Christian leader in what is now the nation of Turkey, was very familiar with this ancient Jewish tradition. Said to be exiled to the island of Patmos by the Romans because of his strong opposition to the emperor cult, the author, a Jewish member of the Jesus movement, wrote to encourage his fellow members who were subjected to sporadic and severe persecution during the latter part of the first century of the Christian era. Many of them were terrified. They saw only death as the end to their suffering at the hands their neighbors and of the imperial authorities. Some defected.

John, drawing heavily from the visions of Ezekiel and Daniel, passages in Isaiah, and from Greek mythology familiar to his readers, wrote to assure his fellow Christians that their sufferings were not in vain and that it was finally God, not Caesar, who would bring an end to their sufferings and reward them for their faithfulness. Given the times, it is hardly surprising that some Christians, even then, read the book as a prediction of the End Times, the second coming of the Messiah, to destroy the wicked and then to redeem the whole world. The End Times had been part of the expectation of the Jesus movement since its beginning.

Since the first century, nearly every major war, epidemic, volcanic explosion or earthquake has prompted some Christians to believe that a particular event in their time was the beginning of the End Times. Yet the book of Revelation has had a troubled history in the life of the church. It was not even included in the earliest canons of the New Testament. Even after it began to be included, leaders of the church viewed it with suspicion. In the fourth century, Bishop Cyril of Jerusalem actually forbade Christians to read the book either in public or in private. Augustine warned against the use of the book to predict the future. Neither Luther, nor Calvin, nor Zwingli thought it worthy of much consideration, and the lectionary of the Greek Orthodox Church omits Revelation completely. Church leaders throughout Christian history have warned against the use of the images and legends in Revelation to predict the End Times, citing Jesus' own words that not even the angels in heaven know when he will come again.

In Wink's view, Jesus certainly envisioned a future of God's reign dramatically breaking into the world even now. In other words, Jesus certainly had an *eschatological* perspective. He believed that the reign of God that had already entered history was clearly in opposition to all unjust and dominant powers that exploited the weak and resorted to violence to maintain power and control. This is a view that is oriented toward the future of humanity and a call to live as if that world is coming and will come—what Wolfhart Pannenberg's work promotes as "proleptic" living.[4] In other words, Wink would have us distinguish between a "positive" and a "negative" apocalyptic. Proponents of both views expect that God will judge the wicked. Yet, the positive apocalyptic believes that not only will evil fall before God's judgment, but that a new order will come with new possibilities for victim *and* oppressor. It is what Desmond Tutu called the only possibility for Christians in a time of wide despair. We cannot succumb to pessimism, he said, nor can we

---

4. See, for example, Pannenberg, *Systematic Theology*, 1:207–15.

possibly pretend to be optimistic. What is left for us is only hope.[5] And that is what lay behind the miracle of South Africa—a region in which Walter Wink has had some experience!

Walter Wink, then, like most of his fellow New Testament scholars, has raised his voice in opposition to the contemporary fascination with apocalyptic interpretation that began with Hal Lindsey and Carol Carlson's book, *The Late Great Planet Earth,* and rose to the level of apocalyptic frenzy after 9/11 and the publication of the "Left Behind" series. Those thirteen books by Timothy LaHaye and Jerry B. Jenkins have already sold more than 70 million copies.

This apocalyptic frenzy has influenced American politics in very dangerous ways. I mention just a few:

1. *Preoccupation with the End Times cuts the nerve of social conscience. It drives us to ignore very real human problems and to absolve ourselves from any responsibility for dealing with them.* No one can doubt that there is enough happening to move all of us to sense a very serious time of limits, a Time of Endings. Global threats such as mounting deaths from malnutrition, uncontrollable disease epidemics, overpopulation, spreading wars, the availability of weapons of mass destruction, the destruction of our air, water and land—this leaves little doubt in our minds about the vulnerability of our beloved world and its people. But who can forget the pronouncement of our former Secretary of the Interior, James Watt. A declared fundamentalist and apocalyptic, Watt once remarked that environmental degradation and clear cutting of forests were not serious problems because Jesus was coming again in the near future, and the whole world would be destroyed and made new anyway. This sort of thinking is pathetic, and when there are real dangers to our world, it is frightening.

2. *Preoccupation with the end times promotes the identification of good and evil people and nations.* This is especially a problem for our own country. Our history began with a claim that we were a new Jerusalem. The bow of the Mayflower had hardly touched the sands of Plymouth before we claimed to be a city set on a hill to be a light to all the nations. Such a claim by and for any nation, and certainly in the case of the United States, threatens to co-opt Jesus' word of "blessing" to those who

5. See, for example, Tutu, *God Has a Dream.*

choose mercy, peace, and justice and transform it into an apocalyptic framework which threatens to shape foreign policy in dangerous ways. It leads us to impose political and economic policies on other nations that are not at all appropriate and often destructive for them. It infuses our thinking with pride, with a patriotism that is totally uncritical. This is a national sin, a sin of pride and arrogance that has led us too often to see our nation as an exception, an island of righteousness in a sea of corruption. This national self-congratulation does not do honor to America. And as the sin of pride, it contradicts our own Christian faith traditions.

3. *Identifying ourselves as the good, the chosen of God gives permission to fanatical patriots to foment hate against our Arab neighbors and Muslims all over the world.* At its heart, this is not true patriotism. It is a frontal attack on the spirit of American democracy. And it is an affront to Christian ideals of toleration and compassion.

4. *When we identify our national enemies as the enemies of God, we begin to sacrifice our liberty in the interest of security, leading to indiscriminate attacks on civil liberties.* This is absolutely contrary to our highest democratic ideals. It is not only unfair. It is un-American.

5. *And finally, when the claim is made that only Christians of a certain type of belief are to be saved from destruction in the End Times, some Christians become arrogant about our knowledge of God.* Christian arrogance about our knowledge of God, in turn, breeds a divisive Christian exclusivism, an exclusivism that has no real basis in our faith and makes inter-religious respect and understanding impossible. And this is not in the spirit of The Human Being, Jesus Christ.

For all these reasons, I am grateful to Walter Wink and other New Testament Scholars who urge that Christians abandon their preoccupation with predicting the End Times. Not only is it an exercise in futility, it is a morally wrong. Indeed, if I understand Jesus, and Walter, it is simply inhuman. It leads us not to paths of righteousness, but to self-righteousness. It leads us not to do justice; it leads us to deny justice. And that is contrary to the mission and meaning of Jesus Christ.

20

The Christ of Mere Literature

Jack Miles

How does a mythic or literary Jesus "work"? And does he
work well enough to still be a catalyst of transformation?
 —Walter Wink

RATHER THAN PURSUE EITHER THE JESUS OF HISTORY OR THE CHRIST of faith, I have sought in my writing on the Gospels to pursue the Jesus Christ of literature—that is, the literary character in whom ancient writers artfully combined the historical memory of Jesus of Nazareth and the Christ of their own literary inventions. One cannot say, I think: "If Jesus had not lived, he would have had to be invented." The likelier admission should be that if Jesus had never lived, no one could ever have invented him. The contribution of the historical Jesus himself, then, to the originality of the Jesus myth was and is indispensable. And yet in the end it is no more than a contribution. The character who lives on in world-historical memory and imagination remains an artful composite.

We are all accustomed by now to seeing the three synoptic Gospels as subtly, self-consciously different composites of shared materials and to seeing the canonical quartet as a composition joining these three to the irradiating power of the Gospel of John. The impulse to which Tatian responded earliest and most directly, the impulse to harmonize the four, has never faded in either the secular or the religious West, and that impulse is better understood as artistic than as documentary in inspiration. But when Jesus Christ is seen as the product rather than the producer of all this harmonization, as the composition rather than the composer, what becomes of his power to "catalyze transformation," in Walter Wink's phrase? Can he still mediate Christian confrontation with "the powers that be"? This is the challenging question that Wink would pose to all merely literary appropriations of Jesus.

Fiction is not real in the sense in which fact is real. Historians aspire to create a common, factual account of the past and to make this account inseparable from a target community's understanding of the present. By this inseparability, past fact, once established, can become the premise for present action. On more than one occasion, historians have succeeded in this literally revolutionary ambition. Why else would historical debate engage political power to the extent that it does?

And yet fiction has a power that fact lacks. Abraham Lincoln is said to have greeted Harriet Beecher Stowe, author of *Uncle Tom's Cabin*, with the exclamation: "So you're the little woman who wrote the book that started this great war!" The account may be apocryphal, but the point remains valid. No assemblage of damning facts about American slavery, all of which after two criminal centuries lay in plain view by the 1860s, did what the little woman's novel did to catalyze liberation.

The historical Jesus himself may well have appreciated this truth better than New Testament historians typically have done. I have long been struck by the fact that Luke 10:29–37 is referred to by critics of all persuasions as the *parable* of the good Samaritan. The Greek word *parabolē* does not occur in the pericope, nor does any other phrase suggesting comparison, such as the familiar "The kingdom of heaven is like . . . ." Why might Jesus not be speaking of the actual, perhaps recent rescue of a wounded man by a generous Samaritan? If he were, I ask, would the reported behavior of this "historical good Samaritan" have been greater in catalyzing a transformation in first-century relations between Jews and Samaritans than the merely imagined behavior that this story has always been taken to enshrine? Perhaps so, but we must immediately note that the story of a historical good Samaritan could not include the priest and the Levite who pass the unconscious victim without helping him. The inclusion of these two figures requires an omniscient narrator, and history does not come with an omniscient narrator, only with a cautious and conscientious reporter. Moreover, the inclusion of the priest and the Levite, besides giving the episode its moral, gives it the familiar tripartite form of a folk tale. So, although there may have been a "historical kernel" in the parable of the Good Samaritan, the evidence is strong that Jesus—supposing, for the moment, that the historical Jesus did indeed tell this story—has given it literary shape and impact, quite probably adding from his imagination the inherently un-knowable but transformative details of the indifferent priest and Levite. Power was surely at issue—the power of the stronger, more numerous Jews over their weaker, less numerous Samaritan cousins. In "unmasking the power," would Jesus have been better advised to eschew invention and simply allow the scandalous goodness of the rescuing Samaritan to speak for itself?

Those who answer in the affirmative would have counseled Jesus to do with the good Samaritan as they have done with Jesus himself, privileging the truth of history over the verisimilitude of literature. Those who answer in the negative would have applauded the Savior for doing as they do when they take the evangelists' artfully interpretive inventions as seriously as they take the "Jesus event." How much would change, in the impact of this pericope, if rather than Jesus adding a priest and a Levite of his own imagining to some contemporary report of a kindly Samaritan, it should have been Luke or some anonymous ancient writer inventing the entire story and merely attributing it to Jesus? How much transformative power does the story lose when we hold it to be invented by a disciple as a script for "the Jesus character" to speak? Does its subversive power not remain?

I believe it does, but I do not mean to vacate the question as sim-ply trivial. Verisimilitude, the truth of art, is only a step away from what political comedian Stephen Colbert has mocked as "truthiness" in contemporary American discourse. What is the difference between verisimilitude and "spin"? A first-century Jew hearing Jesus tell the story of the good Samaritan might feel as contemporary Israelis do when watching sympathetic coverage of the Palestinians on the BBC. And, by the way, did Harriet Beecher Stowe get the facts about slavery right? Finally, if invention is to be so dignified, where does the process stop? Does the dignity of invention extend beyond the agony in the garden as Luke imagined it to the same agony as filmed by Mel Gibson?

I believe that answers can be framed to all these objections, but providing them would go beyond the scope of this modest tribute to the work of Walter Wink. In lieu of anything more systematic, let me conclude then with a gloss on the word *mere* as applied to literature. I used the phrase "merely literary appropriations of Jesus" above rather as one might hear it in casual classroom conversation. But then in casual classroom conversation one hears reference as well to things that are of "merely historical interest." To the dedicated historian, is anything of "merely historical interest"? We may answer yes, but only if we employ the word *mere* in its now archaic original meaning—namely, "pure." Mere history can be like straight whiskey. It can pack a terrific wallop.

But the same goes for literature. As critic George Steiner has written,

> Characteristic of the great works is that they question *us*, they demand a reaction. The archaic torso of Apollo in Rilke's famous poem tells us, in no uncertain terms: "Du sollst dein Leben ändern."[1]

Steiner is writing of all classics in all media: not just literature, but also sculpture. But the confrontation that he describes is very like, is it not, the one that Walter Wink imagines occasioned by the recovered memory of the defiant historical Jesus. Confrontation can be mediated in Wink's meditatively historical way. But it can be mediated in Steiner's more aesthetic way as well.

Alongside Steiner's remark and a large step closer to the sympathetic study of religion, I would place a comment made in passing by the late Wilfred Cantwell Smith, a scholar of comparative religion and, like Walter Wink, as much a theologian as an historian. Smith wrote:

> Again, the notion of objectivity has grown out of work in the natural sciences, where what one investigates—the external world, objects—is less than man, is in some fashion beneath him and her; where what is known seems legitimately to be subordinated conceptually to the mind that knows. In objective knowledge, accordingly, there has arisen a stress on method—a concept, drawn from the arena of ends and means, that inherently implies that what is known is dominated. (Recently, I heard an academic "professional" in the field of English Literature say that that field constitutes a body of material to be mastered. One might better think in terms of the student's being mastered by it, surely!)[2]

---

1. Steiner, *The Idea of Europe;* 10. Simple translation: "You should change your life."

2. Smith, *Toward a World Theology,* 76.

If the encounter with an ancient text or an ancient statue is religious to the extent that it is an experience of submission rather than
mastery, and if the psychological effect of objective, historical research
upon the researcher is the experience of mastery rather than of submission, then the more the Gospels are engaged as history, the less religious
will be the engagement. An historical critic thinking about the Agony
in the Garden (Luke 22:39ff.), for example, cannot fail to notice—it is
indeed professionally incumbent upon him to notice—that the only
possible witnesses to this scene were reportedly asleep when it occurred.
But thus to think is to abort the aesthetic impact—and I would argue,
the religious impact as well—of one of the most moving scenes in the
entire Bible. By contrast, because even a sophisticated literary critic is
required—again, by the criteria of the profession—to respect the truth
of feigned history (Auden's definition of fiction), the experience of being
questioned by the text (Steiner) or mastered by it (Smith) seems more
easily within reach.

I do not wish to make the opposition between historical and aesthetic modes of appropriation sharper that it deserves to be. The two
are not mutually exclusive in every instance. Pedantic criticism can kill,
and magisterial history can thrill. Nor do even the most professional
historians, literary critics, or scientists operate as such 24 hours a day.
We may be fully engaged by more than one role. To paraphrase the great
T-Bone Walker, Saturday's player is Sunday's churchgoer.[3]

To close on a (more conventionally) theological note, the notion
that when God *really* wanted to say something, he would say it through
an historical event rather than through a poem or a tale—in other words,
through some writer's "mere" invention—is, to say the least, theologically presumptuous. Who are we to say? Theological humility, to say
nothing of any other consideration, would seem to dictate extending as
much reverence to sacred art as to sacred history.

3. Walker, "Call it Stormy Monday."

21

Engaging Walter Wink's Powers
—an Activist's Testimony

Alastair McIntosh

A Grounded Theology

THERE IS MORE TO BEING A THEOLOGIAN THAN JUST BEING A THINKER. Speaking as an activist I find myself left malnourished by those theologians who are only great thinkers. To the considerable convenience of our ego self and its love of being clever and in control, thinking on its own cultivates only the "head" part of our psyches. But the activist for social, ecological and spiritual justice in this world must be concerned equally with the "hand"—with doing things. That imperative of involvement makes things very interesting, because it forces realization that it also takes the "heart" to pump blood to both head and hand. Without such engagement of feeling, of emotion, and of metaphysically grounded values, all else is asphyxiated. That was why Jesus insisted that the realm of the divine is found not in the cleverness of all the world, but in the human heart. It is the hardest but most important spiritual lesson we can ever learn, and especially important for those of us who face the latter-day Pharisaic temptations that can go with being academics!

It is this deep engagement—firing on all three cylinders of the troika of head, heart and hand—that draws the engaged person fully into life incarnate. That is why I personally consider that to be a theologian one must be an activist, and being an activist, as I will suggest in this paper, can equally draw us in to theology. Engagement in activism forces the ego self, if I might call it that, to face up to its counterpoint in the shadow self. To put that in plain language, when we're up to the elbows in the doodoo of the world we have to face our own doodoo too! We have to recognise that we're dealing with realities that can either be left to stink in the basement of the individual and collective shadow self, or be processed into rich compost from which new life can grow. And that new life is the fruit of compassion. We get there by iteratively grounding all other parts of ourselves in the deep Self or Godself– in what we Quakers call "that of God in all"—in Buddha-nature, or, as our Hindu fellow humankind would have it, in Atman (individual self) ultimately as Brahman (universal self). St Paul on one of his better days put it all in perspective when he said, "I live, yet not I, but Christ lives within me." Jesus may have been a man in historical time and space; but Christ, in the eternal pleroma, beyond male and female, beyond Jew or Greek, beyond slave and free, is the seed of God in all things (Gal. 3:28).

What I find so exciting with activism is the way it pushes us to deepen into the *Godspace* as I call it—into the realm of God that expresses community with one another, with nature, and in the psychospiritual realm of our inner selves. It provides the power and the courage, as the Psalmist said, to fear no ill (Ps. 23). Speaking personally, I didn't start out from that position. I started out as a teenage activist thirty years ago as an agnostic. Many things transformed that position. But one of the most important was encountering the work of an American theologian named *Walter Wink.*

Rethinking Christianity

I still remember the moment it happened. We were sitting in Peace House—a project of the Quakers and the Iona Community—and listening to Helen Steven, who was then Justice and Peace worker for the Iona Community. I had been drawn to Helen years earlier while on the Isle of Iona because she was open to alternative theologies including feminist, ecological and neopagan perspectives. These were important to me because the religion I'd grown up with—mostly mainstream fundamentalist Scots Presbyterianism—did not speak to my condition. I could not accept its cornerstone of the blood atonement theory of the crucifixion. To die for love—yes. That is what many great lovers of humankind have been called to do in their activism both within and outside of the Christian tradition. But to die because the God of love required it out of angry vindication—that, as I saw it, and from an early age, was a heresy.

Since my late teens I had been on a long spiritual journey. I had abandoned Christianity and found meaning in other faiths, mainly Eastern ones. And then one day in the late 1980s I found myself sitting in Peace House when Helen said that she and Ellen, her partner, were "starting to re-think the whole Christian thing." Why? Because, she said, they had encountered this wonderful work by somebody with the mischievous sounding name of "Walter Wink." She said that his work was of profound importance to activism, and especially nonviolent activism, because it took the understanding of power into realms deeper than she had ever previously encountered in theological writing. "The Powers that Be are Good. But the Powers are fallen. Yet the Powers can be redeemed to their higher, God-given vocation." That was the essence of it. And with that essence was provided a practical formula for activist application. The name of the game is to, 1) Name the Powers . . . finding the courage to break silence and simply state the abuse of power. 2) Unmask the Powers . . . revealing the social, economic, psychological, and spiritual dynamics by which they oppress. 3) And finally, engage the Powers—wrestling so as not to destroy them—not to take life—but rather, to call them back to their higher, God-given calling.

Central to this was a cosmology of power in which "spirituality" is seen by Walter Wink as being the "interiority"—or "angel"—of people, institutions and even nations. As such, the inner life or the life of "prayer" takes on new meaning. Here is how he puts it in one of the most engaging passages from *Engaging the Powers*:

> Those who pray do so not because they believe certain intellectual propositions about the value of prayer, but simply because the struggle to be human in the face of suprahuman Powers requires it. The act of praying is itself one of the indispensable means by which we engage the Powers. It is, in fact, that engagement at its most fundamental level, where their secret spell over us is broken and we are re-established in a bit more of that freedom which is our birthright and potential. Prayer is . . . the interior battlefield where the decisive victory is first won, before engagement in the outer world is even attempted. If we have not undergone that inner liberation, whereby the individual strands of the nets in which we are caught are severed, one by one, our activism may merely reflect one or another counterideology of

some counter-Power. We may simply be caught up in a new collective passion, and fail to discover the transcendent possibilities of God pressing for realization here and now. Unprotected by prayer, our social activism runs the danger of becoming self-justifying good works, as our inner resources atrophy, the wells of love run dry, and we are slowly changed into the likeness of the Beast.[1]

Dharma and the Battlefield

For my taste, the first two volumes of Walter's trilogy—*Naming the Powers* and *Unmasking the Powers* were too conventionally religious to speak to me at that time. But the third, *Engaging the Powers*, totally blew my mind. It is the most important activist's handbook that I have ever encountered—the one that I use as a central text with my students of human ecology who take my masters-level module in Spiritual Activism at Strathclyde University here in Scotland. What Walter's work did for me was that it opened a door on the structure of reality. I am reminded, in saying this, of the very first verse of the Hindu gospel, the *Bhagavad Gita*. Juan Mascaró's beautiful translation for Penguin Classics renders this: "On the field of Truth, on the battlefield of life, what came to pass, Sanjaya. . . ."

As Indian commentators tell, there is just so much packed into those few words. The battlefield is metaphorical. It is "of life," and it rests in Truth or "Dharma" as the Sanskrit has it. Dharma is the opening of God's way; the unfolding of reality such as we recognise in Christian process theology. If one imagines the "Word" or *Logos* of John's gospel, "in the beginning," and booming out to roll through all time—well, that's like the Hindu Dharma. That is what composes the big picture, the stage on which all our worldly activities are played out. And Sanjaya in the Hindu epic is the eagle-eyed charioteer to the blind king, Dhritarashtra. That symbolises the same point that Walter repeatedly makes: the political power of the world is invariably fallen and therefore, to varying degrees, blind. The king—which is to say, I and thou in our small selves—need the charioteer's inner vision of the Godself. This was what Walter's work woke up in me—this radical grounding of reality in Truth that seeks to animate, inspire and guide our action in the world.

1. Wink, *Engaging the Powers*, 297–98.

It lifted me from seeing spirituality as being something transcendent and made it real and effective as something immanent too. It gave new meaning to the sayings and witness of Jesus, and like my friend Helen, helped me to embrace afresh the depth of what it can mean to be "Christian." That didn't mean dumping all the insights gained from other faiths. It just meant recognising that the Holy Spirit may have worked in many ways in many places and times in history, and that wherever love is, God is, too.

Real-life Application

Part of my struggle with Christianity as a younger man is that I always was, and still am, impressed with the empirical claims of science. However, the discovery of mysticism showed me that spiritual life is profoundly empirical too. Even if I myself had never had a direct experience of God, there are plenty of anecdotes around, and when you collect enough anecdotes together they become "data." This recognition helps to silence the bickering of the "head" and allow for an experimental opening of living from the "heart" in the activism of the "hand." For me, this came about in a number of sustained bouts of activist work, the most important of which have been my work with land reform, with environmental protection, with the military and with consumerism. I shall describe the first two of these and briefly mention the others, but let me, first, cite another piece of Walter's insight. It's a passage from *The Human Being*—a book whose importance I was alerted to by my friend, James Jones, the Anglican Bishop of Liverpool. For me, coming from a Scottish bardic culture, this passage profoundly deepens my grip on the tangibility of the spiritual. It helps to legitimise the reality of inner life such as a secular world would otherwise dismiss as being "imaginary."

> Feuerbach had himself said, "Imagination is the original organ of religion," but he was unable to grasp the positive meaning of his insight. . . . The realm of the imagination, or what I prefer to call, following Henry Corbin, the imaginal realm, produces a third kind of knowing, intermediate between the world of ideas, on the one hand, and the object world of sense perception on the other. The imaginal possesses extension and dimension, figures and colours, but lacks full materiality and hence cannot be perceived by the senses. In dreams and visions, for example, we perceive the action *as if* it were staged on the physical plane, but

it is not. This intermediate world of images and archetypes can be known only by the "transmutation of inner spiritual states into outer states, into vision-events symbolizing with these inner states" [Corbin]. Concrete symbolization, such as temples, rituals, and myths, may help us to find our interiority outside ourselves, as Henry Corbin puts it. We may falsely assume that these images are subjective creations of our psyches, or pseudo-objective delusions, like hallucinations. But we do not make all of them up. We imagine them, to be sure, but something real evokes our imagination. . . . Unless the imagination is recognized as autonomous to a high degree, we trivialize the divine encounter. We do not simply create God with our images; rather, our images are precipitated not only from deep within us, but from beyond our personal unconscious. Medieval Jewish mystics called that place "the roots of the soul"—a deep, underground world of archetypes that has encoded the experience of the species from the beginning. It is the recovery of the imaginal that makes possible both the reenchantment of nature and the recovery of soul, in ourselves and in things.[2]

I suppose that the importance of that passage for one with a disposition for Jungian psychology is that it provides flesh to the activist dictum that "the personal is the political." It allows us to bridge inner and outer space, and as Walter suggests in the first passage that I quoted from him, it renders seamless "outer" activism and "inner" prayer life. This helps to keep open the doorways of compassion. As the American spiritual teacher Ram Dass says, it helps us to do what we have to do with people but to keep our hearts open to them. Put another way, Jesus saw that as activists we would make many enemies, but he recommended trying to love them. Such an attitude renders our adversaries "worthy adversaries" because, not least, they become participants with us in a cosmology of interconnection. Shakespeare said that "all the world's a stage," and this kind of thinking empowers us to see our activism as being not just social, political, environmental, doctrinal or whatever, but more importantly, to see it as a kind of medieval mystery play in which the name of the game of what gets played out before people during a campaign is nothing less than the revelation of God. Our activism in issues of ordinary life therefore becomes a form of mission: the articulation of spiritual vision. In other words, spiritual activism both sustains

2. Wink, *The Human Being*, 40–41.

those of us who engage in it and teaches those around us some of the meanings of spirituality.

In 2003, thanks to the very great thoughtfulness and kindness of my friend, James Cashen, in upper New York State, I had the privilege of meeting Walter and his wife June. It was clear to me during this meeting at his home that part of Walter's strength comes from his spiritual marriage, and the sense of the divine feminine that June embodies both in her presence and in her beautiful work as a potter. The morning that we spent together gave me the opportunity to ask Walter to clarify something about how he uses the word, "spiritual." I put it to him that he tends to use it mainly to imply the "interiority" of things, but that another use would be to imply that of God in things—the meanings of love as the process of coming alive to the aliveness of life. He agreed that both usages are valid and that, at a deep level, they connect. For me, such radical "spirituality" is the ultimate ballgame on the activist stage. Let me now briefly describe some of these applications.

Case Study 1: Scottish Land Reform

The work for which I am best known is my contribution to modern land reform in Scotland. In 1991, four of us set up a psychological challenge to landed power. Land ownership is an issue in Scotland that goes back to the 18th and 19th century "Highland Clearances" in which the people were forced off land that had been turned into a commodity—valued no longer for how many people it could support, but for the profit it could generate. Today, nearly two-thirds of the private land in Scotland is controlled by just 1,000 owners. The challenge that we levelled was to set up a land trust with the stated aim of bringing the Isle of Eigg into community ownership. We had no money at the outset—simply a vision, and an understanding that even more than being a legal hold, land ownership is a psychospiritual one on the resources and minds of the people who live on the land. Many big landowners in Scotland see the land, according to my analysis, not just in economic terms but also as a way to bolster their ontological insecurity. They have land in order to be somebody. As such, and consistent with the second temptation of Christ in Luke's rendition, big landowners take on kingdoms idolatrously (Luke 4:5-8). This damages community integrity.

The owner of Eigg had been forced by the courts to place the island on the market in the aftermath of divorce proceedings. He described the island as "a collector's item" and we reasoned that we could challenge the "interiority" of that perspective, thus causing a bit of market spoiling. Consistent with Gutiérrez's emphasis on liberation theology being conducted from the underside of history—by telling the story of the oppressed—we created a situation where the typical rich buyer, looking for a hideaway place of retreat—would be put off. The natives were restless, so who'd want to holiday there! It was a very simple formula and one that I sought to legitimise by overtly using land-based liberation theology, such as I describe throughout my book, *Soil and Soul*.[3]

The outcome of this and many other contributions from a great many other people, and primarily the island residents themselves, was that the island stuck on the market. The community increasingly grew in its own confidence and reclaimed hope. Eventually, it raised three million dollars from some ten thousand donations from around the world, and Eigg was brought into community land ownership in June 1997.

More than that, Eigg also set a pattern and example for others. Its success contributed to the Scottish Parliament passing the Land Reform Scotland Act as flagship legislation in 2003. At the time of writing in summer 2007, we now have an astonishing 367,000 acres of Scotland that have been brought under community control, and this represents fully 2% of the Scottish land mass.

Mainstream Scottish churches played an important role in the legitimisation process that led to this transformation, or, as its critics like to call it, "the Mugabification of Scotland"! For example, the Church of Scotland, the Free Church of Scotland, the Scottish Episcopal Church and the Scottish Churches Parliamentary Office all set up commissions that provided input to the land reform process by developing an applied land theology. My voice was only one of many, but it was a voice that was heard, and behind it lay the applied theology of our dear friend and venerated teacher, Walter Wink.

3. McIntosh, *Soil and Soul*.

Case Study 2: the Isle of Harris Superquarry

At the same time as the Eigg Trust was getting going, a multinational corporation announced that it had acquired mineral rights in the National Scenic Area on the Isle of Harris, near my home area in the Outer Hebrides of Scotland.

I had recently returned from working in Papua New Guinea. There the Bougainville crisis had alerted me to the problems that massive mining projects can cause for indigenous communities and fragile ecosystems. I therefore joined those who were opposing the quarry, though it looked like a hopeless task.

My role was publicly to name, unmask and engage the principalities and the powers behind the quarry. Naming meant making visible the scar that this would create on both the landscape and the community, including invocation of such designations as Mammon and Moloch to describe the "spirit" behind what was proposed. Unmasking meant exegeting, in articles and public talks, why this was being done and how it might affect the life of the community. And engaging was tackling the corporation, especially through the media but also through their local supporters, asking if a quarry was really the God-given calling for the exquisite beauty of the Isle of Harris.

For the first three years these arguments cut very little ice. But in 1994, the government public inquiry opened. Its terms of reference included cultural considerations. I argued at the pre-inquiry meeting that this should include spiritual considerations as Harris is a profoundly Presbyterian community. I pointed out that in the *Institutes* Calvin refers to the "beautiful theater" of creation that reveals the majesty of God (*Inst.* III:XIV:20).

There was a need to bring zest into the campaign. We needed something that would make more visible the inner spirituality of the situation. This crystallised when an American friend introduced me to the then Warrior Chief of the Mi'Kmaq Nation in Nova Scotia. He had prevented a similar superquarry on *Kluscap*—their sacred mountain on Cape Breton Island. As again is described in *Soil and Soul*, I managed to persuade him to come and testify in the Scottish inquiry and to do so not just with myself, but also with the Rev. Professor Donald Macleod of the Free Church College—one of Scotland's leading theologians.[4]

4. McIntosh, *Soil and Soul*, 196–247.

The combination of a Calvinist professor, a Quaker heretic and a pagan Indian chief (as the newspapers put it) was just too good to be true for the media, and the sleepy public inquiry was catapulted into the international limelight. But more than that, while the media were bemused by the theology, they nonetheless reported reasonably accurately on it. That got a lot of people thinking more deeply about values.

The outcome was that all this and more than I can relate here caused long procedural delays. The corporation's flagship project started to founder, and with it, their share price fell. This caused the English company as it was, Redland, to be taken over by an even bigger French one, Lafarge. In 2004 I was able successfully to broker Lafarge's withdrawal from what, by that time, was a nearly-wrecked flagship. But there was one further irony to all this. Lafarge came back to me and challenged me on my own complicity with the powers! "We all use quarry products," they said to me, "so will you help us to do so more responsibly?" The consequence is that I now sit, unpaid, on their environmental advisory board and meet regularly with the top management of a company that as the world's biggest manufacturer of cement, is responsible for fully 1% of the world's emissions of carbon dioxide to the atmosphere. I am proud to be able to report that they are now winning acclaim for having reduced the level of these emissions per ton of cement produced by 14% on 1990 levels. It may not be enough to save the world but, to me, it suggests something about human nature. It suggests, as Walter tells us, that the Powers are Good; the Powers are fallen; but the Powers can be redeemed to a higher, God-given vocation.

Other Examples of Application

These are just two of the ways that Walter's insights have inwardly fortified and informed my own work. Another example is my work with the military. Every year for the past decade I have been invited to lecture on nonviolence to four hundred senior officers from some seventy countries on the Advanced Command & Staff Course at Britain's foremost school of war—the Joint Services Command & Staff College. They get a full on blast of Water Wink, and at times I have been given standing ovations and told that they are now able to respect nonviolence even if they do not agree with it. Some 4,000 senior military have thereby been exposed to the idea of naming, unmasking and engaging the Powers that Be!

Another example is with my work on advertising—especially that of tobacco companies. This has been featured in the front page lead article of the *Wall Street Journal* as well as the *Sunday Times*.[5] Basically, my technique has been to inquire into the nature of the powers underlying Gallaher's advertisements. My conclusion—as can be read online by Googling "cigarette adverts" or "Silk Cut"—is that the spirit of death itself has been recruited to market the ecstasy of destruction. In a book that I am currently writing about the psychology and spirituality underlying climate change, I am using this work as an icon into the spirit of consumerism and what J. K. Galbraith referred to as "wants creation." I am suggesting that if we want to live sustainably with our planet, we need nothing less than a new heart and a new mind, redeemed to higher God-given vocation from the fall into the idolatry of consumerism. Again, Walter's guiding hand in where I am coming from will be evident.

Gratitude

I always think that there is a direct relationship between a student's ability to feel gratitude to a teacher and that student's capacity to learn. In the East it is encoded as "respect for the teacher," but that is too rigid a construct to capture the imaginations of most of us in this post-sixties era. I think we need to go deeper, and I remember seeing a review of Walter's work where some bishop or another had said, "God has blessed the writing of this book." For me, sitting at the feet of Walter's work from across the other side of the great Atlantic Ocean has been to receive a very profound blessing. In my campaigns, and especially during the difficult times and during all the failures, I have felt Walter's hand on my shoulder even before I ever met him face to face. I have felt touched by the spirit of God in what Walter has revealed unto me (and that use of Biblical language is deliberate). All this has moved onwards and outwards into the world. It has taken many different forms, dressed up variously as activism, academia and just the simplicity of ordinary life. And so, thank you, dear June and dear Walter, for what you have

5. Parker-Pope, "No Butts About It"; Mega, "Cigarette Ads May Induce Death Wish."

given to me and to us all. You have helped to kindle the fire of love made manifest. You have touched the lives of many who you will never know nor they you. But all, whether they know it or not, have been touched by the divine. Again, thank you, and God bless you both.

22

From the Past to the Future
of Biblical Activism

Bill Wylie-Kellermann

WHEN I WAS A STUDENT AT UNION, SOME THIRTY YEARS AGO, WALTER Wink was my Introduction to New Testament instructor. Not only that, but my small group was convened not by one of his graduate students now gone on to repute of his or her own, but by Walter himself. One day, during a Bible study—Matthew's text on the treasure in the field and the pearl of great price—Walter halted the discussion while we all went around the circle and responded each to a question he had put: For what are you willing to die? I suspect I'd be embarrassed to remember my answer. Happily I don't. But I do recall the question, more or less constantly. I try to live with it. I don't believe anyone should be permitted to graduate seminary, never mind be baptized, without being confronted with that question.

This was in the same period when Wink wrote *The Bible in Human Transformation*,[1] wherein he exorcized from himself the imperial naïveté of detached objectivism. Our seminar go-round could well characterize the interrogatory hermeneutic he was developing. In the end, it is the text that interrogates us. To take seriously Walter Wink's work (never mind the Gospels themselves) is to be summoned to a level of engagement, risk, and transformation—both personal and political.

I write and work as a biblical activist, and my personal reflection here is filtered largely through Walter's three books known as the "powers trilogy," which deal with the three practices of naming, unmask-

---

1. Wink, *The Bible in Human Transformation*. His popularized sequel to it outlining a new paradigm was *Transforming Bible Study*.

ing, and engaging the powers that be.[2] *Engaging the Powers* is truly the *magnum opus*; a piece of work which moves the project beyond pulling the principalities and powers back onto the map of social ethics, and constructs in essence a new or renewed theology of nonviolence, reinventing it by way of the scriptures. Put another way, this is a theology which links the vocational witness of the church with the transforming power of non-violence. Happily for pastors, this stuff will preach. And for activists, it will play.

My own sustained and formative exposure to a theology of the powers came in the context of faith-grounded resistance to nuclear weapons. I first read *Naming the Powers* in jail, and I revisited it, in conjunction with *Engaging the Powers,* during another two-month stint after a liturgical trespass at the Strategic Air Command base in northern Michigan. These books resonated with urgency, as I realized that I was actually comprehending the demonic powers inherent in nuclearism and its institutional complex. They pointed toward the blasphemous presumptions of sovereignty in history, framed as a first-strike (today we say pre-emptive) nuclear doctrine and the political rites of empire. They helped explain and nourish the fact that the much of the clearest public opposition took form as liturgical direct action[3]—praying in forbidden places or ritually unmaking weapons as an act of right worship.[4]

However, one of my early experiments with Wink's material was more urban in character. I had gathered a small circle of Detroit pastors and community activists for bible study, social historical analysis, and (one might say) poetic discernment. Making a small leap from Walter's

2. Actually, Wink has done at least six books related to the powers. In addition to the trilogy: *Naming the Powers, Unmasking the Powers,* and *Engaging the Powers,* he has also written *Cracking the Gnostic Code, When the Powers Fall,* and *The Powers That Be,* this latter being a popular summary of the "trilogy."

3. One of my own books, *Seasons of Faith and Conscience: Kairos, Confession, Liturgy,* was an attempt, drawing on Wink, to articulate theologically and historically these efforts.

4. I am thinking here of the Plowshares movement. The first of these, the Plowshares Eight, took place September 9, 1980, at the General Electric weapons plant in King of Prussia, Pennsylvania. Daniel Berrigan's reflection on his part in that action which appeared in the *Catholic Worker* (October 1980) was republished in Art Laffin and Anne Montgomery, eds., *Swords Into Plowshares: Nonviolent Direct Action for Disarmament.* Laffin is the chronicler of such disarmament actions and periodically publishes updated accounts. See, for example, Laffin, *Swords Into Plowshares: A Chronology of Plowshares Disarmament Actions 1980–2003.*

reading of the "angels of the churches" and the "angels of the nations," we set out to treat the city as a creature with a life and integrity of its own. In the end, we produced letters addressing the Spirit of Detroit which named its character and choices in a concrete historical moment.[5] Among those who sat with this circle, Grace Lee Boggs, the organic intellectual community activist,[6] has ever since spoken of her work as "reviving, rebuilding, and respiriting" Detroit from the ground up.

Over the years since then, it dawned upon me how significant those sessions were in laying the foundation for participation in the Detroit newspaper strike of 1995. A number of the same folks ended up being the core of Readers United, an independent citizens group that attempted to support the strikers by reframing the struggle as a community-based non-violent campaign. We were also in a position to organize direct action, which the unions (and their lawyers) were too timid to employ. What strikes me is how both the framing and the tactics were implicitly shaped by Wink's theology of the powers.

The accountability of the Detroit Newspaper Agency to the judgment of God is one example of what Wink calls the "vocation" of the powers. This vocation is an *assigned* vocation—assigned to the powers, in the service of human life within the community. This is their identity in creation; it is who they are called to be through the Word of God. Just how this plays out in specific instances is a very radical concern which Christians in the work of discernment are authorized to address. What is the vocation of a bank, for example? How is it called concretely to serve human life? Or in this case, what is the vocation of a newspaper? What is it for? Which is also to say, how is this calling violated, in newspapers' contempt for its own workers, for the culture of a union town, for its own readership?

Once, speaking at a street rally, I asked the picketers and protesters if they had ever read the face of the Detroit News Building, and pointed upwards to the ledge. High above the stage and the street, nearly out of sight and entirely out of mind, were to be seen etched in stone a series of epithets, among them: Friend of Every Righteous Cause, Reflector of Every Human Interest, Mirror of the Public Mind, Dispeller of Ignorance and Prejudice, Bond of Civic Unity, Protector of Civic

5. See my own account of that effort, Wylie-Kellerman, "Discerning the Angel of Detroit."

6. Boggs, *Living for Change: An Autobiography.*

Rights, Troubler of Public Conscience, Scourge of Evil Doers, Exposer of Secret Iniquities, Unrelenting Foe of Privilege and Corruption, A Light Shining in All Dark Places. After the recitation of each phrase, I would get a great laugh, as the strikers knew the bitter truth in each instance. Their laughter essentially signaled their understanding of "the fall," the distortion, confusion, and inversion, which the powers suffer vocationally.

These phrases written in stone, romantic and pretentious though they be, actually suggest the very bases on which Detroit Newspapers Incorporated is accountable to human life and so also stands before the judgment of God. For some, the former may be easier to swallow theologically than the latter. Yet, just as the prophets brought the nations before the bar of God's judgment—the nations and not the just the kings or the individuals comprising them—so all the powers may be thought likewise subject to the judgment of God. Beneath that summons, we can also discern certain political tactics. Or so Wink suggests.

In practice, Walter Wink has occasioned a revival of discernment as the politically pre-eminent charism. So often the church finds itself in coalition and at table with political groups who have a lucid and well-researched social analysis, generally a materialist read of the moment. For that we can be grateful. But it is half the story at best, as though we were viewing the situation with a half-blind eye, without seeing the invisible *and* the visible, without knowing the depth and perspective which spiritual discernment can bring to bear. A faith community that withholds or suppresses or ignores its gift does the struggle no service. To see at that depth is to alter analysis, timing, and tactics. The United Methodist activist George McClain has written a little volume elaborating these questions, *Claiming All Things for God: Prayer, Discernment, and Ritual for Social Change.*[7]

Walter has also resourced movement activists by collecting and circulating stories of nonviolent action. For over ten years, with Jo Clare Hartsig, he edited a feature in *Fellowship Magazine* which narrated vignettes large and small exemplifying the craft and spirit of nonviolence.[8] One suspects it all began on note cards with illustrations for the

7. McClain, *Claiming All Things for God.*

8. "Nonviolence in the Arena" was regular feature of *Fellowship* from 1993–2005. See also his anthology of writings on nonviolence collected from *Fellowship*: Wink, *Peace is the Way.*

Powers trilogy, but turned into a great stockpile as stories were recovered and rehearsed. For many of us such evidentiary narratives nurture a discipline of hope. The tellings are themselves acts of resistance or transformation.

It was also the Fellowship of Reconciliation (FOR), particularly at the behest of Richard Deats, who sponsored Walter's nonviolent incursion into South Africa at the height of the anti-apartheid struggle. FOR had published a plain-brown-cover version of *Jesus' Third Way* and distributed it to 4,000 black and white pastors. This was a contextually specific version of analysis that would eventually appear in *Engaging the Powers*. It was a road test of the material, so to speak. The circulation was to be followed by a series of retreats, but Walter was unable to get a visa (a measure perhaps of the impact the tract itself was already having). In consequence, he went in illegally through Lesotho. (The nearly mystical providences of that passage are recounted in *The Powers that Be*.) In this he faced not only the authorities, but the risk of being a white outsider evangelizing the biblical gospel of nonviolence. Both man and material stood the test.

Perhaps the strongest measure of Wink's impact is the way his work is finding its way into activist culture. It becomes one with the political vernacular of movement discourse. Within recent memory of this reflection I can tabulate an impressive short list of instances experienced or overheard:

- A Christian Peacemaker Team participant returns from work in Gaza and the West Bank reflecting on her experience through the lens of the "Myth of Redemptive Violence" and Wink's uppity reading of the Sermon on the Mount.

- An Alinsky organizer with Gamaliel cites Wink in connection with understanding power biblically, commending prayer and contemplation to organizers.[9]

- A homiletics professor takes his class to Atlanta for prophetic street preaching and ends up writing a preaching text based on the powers.[10]

9. Jacobsen, *Doing Justice*.

10. Saunders and Campbell, *The Word on the Street*; Campbell, *The Word before the Powers*.

- A panel member at an advance retreat laying the foundations for the Greensboro Truth and Reconciliation Commission draws on the visible/invisible vocational structure of the powers.

- A restorative justice activist freely considers the "angels of the nations" in the work of forgiveness.

- A nationally known anti-racism trainer wants to explore the practical implications of naming racism a demonic power.

- A founder of the Jonah House resistance community addresses a group of Methodist activists in Los Angeles using the terminology of the "domination system," as though this were simply common parlance in movement circles.

Moreover, partly under the sway of Wink's influence, activists are engaging bible study as a spiritual and political discipline, a social practice of analysis and community building. They are attending not just to the prophets or Exodus and gospels, but to the creation narratives, to apocalyptic, to St Paul! One project, with roots in the "underground seminary" conjured by William Stringfellow and Daniel Berrigan in the 70s and 80s, fits well with Wink's movement influence. Now in its sixth year, "Word and World" is a floating institute for faith-grounded movement activists, a school of discipleship which builds biblical and cultural capacity among those committed to social transformation. Along with recovering local movement history and employing popular pedagogies, it relies heavily on a rich variety of bible study, under the conviction that this is an essential tool and even a source of transformative power.

Now comes Wink with *The Human Being*—*magnum opus* giving way to *magnum opus*. This sequel clearly resumes the direct conversation with the biblical guild. It is another turn of the wheel in the grand hermeneutical circle of his life. Since the practical implications are momentous, one waits to imagine how it will spin out engagements more accessible to activists. I think readily of William Stringfellow's short logion of ethical practice: "to live humanly in the face of death . . . ."

It is fitting that Stringfellow be mentioned repeatedly in the conclusion of this reflection. Another circle turns on him. A pre-eminent theologian for activists in his own right, it was his work which seeded Walter Wink's own massive project on the principalities and powers.[11]

11. Wink, "Stringfellow on the Powers," 25. He also identifies there the partially unacknowledged debt he owes to Stringfellow.

Like Wink he had the capacity to witness the demonic in Empire and to name its assault on human life, indeed upon all of creation. I had the blessing to sit in a class that he and Walter taught together twenty years ago at Auburn Seminary. Between the first weekend session and the second, several months later, Stringfellow crossed over into blessed memory. Not, however, before he had the chance to read page proofs for *Naming the Powers*. He confided, "It's going to be a very important work." William Stringfellow was nothing if not prophetic. He proved right. Walter Wink's work is a gift, enormously important in the struggle on a human scale against the globalizing and totalizing powers of death we now confront. It has been important to me personally, as well. So I feel authorized to say on behalf of many, even many to come, *Thank you, dear Friend of us all.*

23

What's Next?

Ray Gingerich

So what's next?—not after Walter, but with Walter. My assignment here is to look into the future—not a future far away, but a tomorrow that is already here. What are the next steps for the community of faith? Our own challenge is to take Walter's contributions and let them be the catalyst, energizer and inspiration to go forward together.

After all that has been said today I have little to contribute that is new. But perhaps metaphoric imagery will evoke further reflection and creativity from us. The imagery emerges from the occasion when "Joshua fit de battle of Jericho."

∾

Walter has brought us into formation around Jericho. We as a community (the army of faith) are surrounding Jericho. *We* are all those who are gathered here today. *We* includes our local communities of faith—wherever we are living—to find and to follow the way of peace. *We* are communities of resistance. Jericho is Domination writ large. Jericho is Empire. Jericho is the Powers fallen.

Walter has called the Powers by their name. In so doing he has begun to unmask them, and we are beginning to see them for what they are. Jericho has become a primary point of orientation. In a kind of perverted way, Jericho, Empire, becomes our GPS—our Global Positioning System. It lets us know where the battle is being fought, what our purpose *is* in the grander scheme of things, and how we are positioned as we move toward our destination.

But day by day, as each day we encircle the city one more time, we have learned from Walter that the Powers, too, have immense sophistication. Even as we surround them, the Powers create new "stealth systems" designed to trip up our spiritual radars and to jam our GPS. There is much about the Powers that is attractive—some would even add, necessary to our security. We have much in common with them. They are, on closer observation, mirroring us. Or is it we who are mirroring them?

The next step to take, then, as we pursue the consequences of Walter's work, is to discern ever anew who we are and who we are becoming—lest in our quest to call the Powers by their names and to engage them, we fall prey to them. This step calls for guidelines beyond the Domination System, the establishing of norms in a nearly normless society, and of a *social identity with communal commitments* that reach well beyond the psychic centeredness of the individual. We need to find a positioning point other than Jericho, other than the culture of Empire. For in the subconscious of our psyches we have seen that the people of Empire have many things; and that they live well. In fact, we sense that quite often they have what we are seeking.

The longer we march around Jericho, the more attractive Jericho becomes. We thought we had a strong, life-affirming self-identity, but now we see that the writers of *our* story—our American story—and the shapers of our worship, just as the writers of the Joshua stories, were myopic and often saw double. Their "prophetic vision" was cast into the framework of democracy and written in the language of servanthood, but between the lines it was self-serving, and to many it has become a seduction myth. As people of faith moving into a new millennium, we knew we were in deep trouble, but when the next election came up our people chose against their better interests. Our people chose the security of Empire—which in the end, like Jericho itself, is self-destructive. Our people chose the greed and the violence of an Emperor who survives by the slaughter of others. We thought Empire was of *them*; but now we know that Empire is among us and within us. To use a quote coming from an African American, that Walter himself has used: "You caint no more give someone something you ain't got than you can come back from somewhere you ain't been."[1] And we, my American friends,

1. Wink, *The Human Being*, 12.

my friends of Western civilization, "free-marketeers" preoccupied with consumption—too often we just ain't got it.

But our task is further complicated and made even more challenging. For if we follow Walter's insights and instructions, our second step is infinitely more complex than it appeared as we approached Jericho.

∾

Our goal is not to destroy the people of Jericho, not even the city. Wink has declared that "The Jesus who died at the hands of the Powers died every bit as much for the Powers as for the people."[2]

Our formation around Jericho is to redeem Jericho! The redemption of Empire! That is what comes out of the work of Wink and must continue to be developed within this legacy. We are called to move beyond techniques that would enable us to get along (i.e., "live peaceably") with Empire. The work of Christ is to redeem the Powers—institutions and Empire. We stand at the very beginning of a hugely challenging task. Virtually all of our theology of the past millennia has focused on the redemption of individuals and psyches, and on groups of individuals. Christian orthodoxy has operated with the mistakenly mythical assumption that if individuals are redeemed then structures will be redeemed. Our theology *and* our institutions have utterly failed to take seriously the fallenness of the Powers and their cultural seductiveness.

Walter's work pushes us not primarily to castigate and to exorcise the Powers—although that too may have its place. Walter is directing us to engage the Powers and by so doing redeem them. This is a whole new step in soteriology. This is a new dimension in the coming of the Kingdom of God. We who have created our Jerichos, we who have participated in the greed, the inequities and the injustices of Empire, are now, under the tutelage of Walter Wink, called upon to transform the very structures undergirding the Powers. Those sacred hierarchical structures must be given new, life-giving, salvific form. We as human beings cannot live without structures, and we are not given the option to start *de novo*. Yet we are not left without hope, for Christ died for the Powers!

I see, for example, my home institution, Eastern Mennonite University, the institution which has been called by one of our Federal

2. Wink, *Engaging the Powers*, 82.

Judges, "the university with a soul," the institution which is showing up on the world map because of its Conflict Transformation Program and its Summer Peacebuilding Institute. Here is a place where each summer for the past ten years people from thirty to fifty of the most strife-torn nations of the world have converged on campus to study peace. To my astonishment, I need not look long to see that even this place is taking its *structural* cues more from General Motors, built on the paradigm of Empire, than from the Sermon on the Mount and Gandhi and Martin Luther King, Jr. Even our "peacebuilding" institutions are structurally in need of Christ's redemption.

So our second step is to think within a new structural and cultural paradigm in which every woman and every man is equally empowered. This will be a non-hierarchical structure, but beyond that we know all too little. For many years now, we have sensed the anomalies in our institutions of redemption, and we have talked about the pieces of more egalitarian structures, but the new paradigm that gets whole peoples to think in radically new social terms and builds a new cultural reality has not yet emerged. And *that* is the challenge to which Walter is calling us when he says that "Jesus who has died at the hands of the Powers, died every bit as much for the Powers as for the people." That is the challenge that faces us in the formation into which Walter has led us—in which we have encompassed Jericho.

But into a future that is already upon us, we follow Walter one more step.

∾

Ours is the challenge to redeem Jericho *nonviolently.*

Nonviolence is not simply a strategy to conquer—when, after the walls fall, we will plunder, ravage and rape. Jericho's redemption lies in the means we use to "conquer" it. Jericho's redemption and Israel's redemption and Iraq's redemption and America's redemption and the church's redemption—these are tasks that need to be pursued step-by-step. But in the end, it is all of one piece. And it can be accomplished only through the costly power of nonviolence. To quote Gandhi:

> Nonviolence is the greatest force humanity has been endowed with. Truth is the only goal humanity has. . . . But Truth cannot be and never will be reached except through nonviolence.

> That which distinguishes humanity from all other animals is our
> capacity to be nonviolent.[3]

And as Walter has so carefully observed and astutely proclaimed in
a multitude of ways, "Jesus revealed to the world for the first time since
the rise of the conquest-states, God's domination-free order of nonviolent love."[4] Nonviolence is the means that keeps us from becoming like
the enemy. It is, therefore, not only the redemption of Empire but of
ourselves, as well as a harbinger of the creation of a domination-freeing
order.

Violence, if ever there was a purpose for it, is in our twenty-first
century, utterly obsolete. Its use carries us ever further toward anni-
hilation. But our institutions, even our peace-and-justice institutions,
are structured much like tiny conquest-states. Ours is the challenge to
take the next steps in doing what Jesus failed to accomplish because the
Powers of Empire and Religion collaborated and killed him.

∽

I do not know how far I can push the imagery of surrounding Jericho,
the Empire of which we are a part; or of redeeming Jericho, which calls
for imaginative and courageous living stretching well beyond the imagination available to us. And all this must be done nonviolently, for that
is the only power claimed by those who are of the domination-freeing
order. It is clear to me that the march for the days ahead will be more
than a sufficient challenge to all of us, and that it calls for all of us to join
in solidarity in spirit, in community and in action.

I want to conclude these reflections with a "thank you" and a prayer.
To Walter, my deepest gratitude for the purpose and direction you have
added to my life and the lives of many others. And now the prayer from
the latest edition of *Fellowship Magazine* (the final edition to be edited
by Richard Deats)—a prayer written by Walter Wink:

> Creator God:
> Give us a heart for simple things:
> Love and laughter, bread and wine,
> Tales and dreams

3. Quoted in Deats, *Mahatma Gandhi*, 36.
4. Wink, *Engaging the Powers*, 45.

Fill our lives with green and growing hope;
Make us a people of Justice
Whose song is Allelujah
And whose name breathes love.[5]

5. Wink, untitled prayer, *Fellowship*, May/June 2005, inside back cover.

24

Parting Prayer

Richard Deats

> Gracious God,
>
> Source of our Hope
>
> Giver of all-encompassing Love

We are particularly grateful for this day of celebration of the profound and wide-ranging impact of the life and work of your servant Walter Wink.

Here, amidst family and friends, colleagues and co-workers, we find ourselves in a community pledged to build a domination-free order. Give us faith to discern the new signs of hope, most often in places least expected.

In the midst of so many blessings, help us to give ourselves anew to engaging the powers and to do so with determination, faith and compassion. Keep us sensitive to the pain and suffering, the injustice and violence in the world.

In Jesus name,

Amen.

Published Works of Walter Wink

Books

John the Baptist in the Gospel Tradition. Society for New Testament Studies Monographs Series 7. Cambridge: Cambridge University Press, 1968. Reprinted, Eugene, OR: Wipf & Stock, 2000.

The Bible in Human Transformation: Toward A New Paradigm for Biblical Study. Philadelphia: Fortress Press, 1973. Translated as *Schriftauslegung als Interaktion.* Stuttgart: Kohlhammer, 1976.

Transforming Bible Study: A Leaders Guide. Nashville: Abingdon, 1980. 2d ed., 1990. Translated as *Bibelarbeit: Ein Praxisbuch für Theologen und Laien.* Stuttgart: Kohlhammer, 1982.

Naming the Powers: The Language of Power in the New Testament. Philadelphia: Fortress, 1984.

Unmasking the Powers: The Invisible Forces That Determine Human Existence. Philadelphia: Fortress, 1986.

Violence and Nonviolence in South Africa. Philadelphia: New Society Publishers, in cooperation with the Fellowship of Reconciliation, 1987. Also published as *Jesus' Third Way: The Relevance of Nonviolence in South Africa Today.* Cape Town: Methodist Publishing House, 1988. Translated as *Angesichts des Feindes: Der Dritte Weg Jesu in Sudafrika und Anderswo.* Munich: Claudius, 1988.

Engaging the Powers: Discernment and Resistance in a World of Domination. Philadelphia: Fortress, 1992.

Cracking the Gnostic Code: The Powers in Gnosticism. Society of Biblical Literature Monograph Series 46. Atlanta: Scholars, 1993.

Proclamation 5: Holy Week, Year B. Minneapolis: Fortress, 1993.

Healing a Nation's Wounds: Reconciliation on the Road to Democracy. Uppsala, Sweden: Life and Peace Institute, 1997. Also published as *When the Powers Fall: Reconciliation on the Road to Democracy.* Minneapolis: Fortress, 1998.

The Powers That Be. New York: Doubleday, 1998. Translated as *De Heersende machten.* Delft, The Netherlands: Meinema, 1999.

The Third Way: Reclaiming Jesus' Nonviolent Alternative. Alkmaar, The Netherlands: International Fellowship of Reconciliation, 1998.

Editor. *Homosexuality and Christian Faith: Questions of Conscience for the Churches.* Minneapolis: Fortress, 1999.

Editor. *Peace Is the Way: Writings on Nonviolence from the Fellowship of Reconciliation.* Maryknoll, NY: Orbis, 2000.

The Human Being: Jesus and the Enigma of the Son of the Man. Minneapolis: Fortress, 2001.

Jesus and Nonviolence: A Third Way. Facets Series. Minneapolis: Fortress, 2003.

Articles and Chapters

1969–1974

"Jesus and Revolution." *Union Seminary Quarterly Review* 25 (1969) 37–59.

"Apocalypse in Our Time." *Katallagete* 3 (Fall 1970) 13–18.

"Jesus as Magician." Review of Clement of Alexandria and a Secret Gospel of Mark and The Secret Gospel. *Union Seminary Quarterly Review* 30 (Fall 1974) 3–14.

"Jesus Named in the Charismatic Movement (Union Theological Seminary January Lecture)." *UTS Journal* (June 1974) 2–4.

1975–1979

"How I Have Been Snagged by the Seat of My Pants While Reading the Bible." *Christian Century* (September 24, 1975) 816–19.

"Jesus Named in the Charismatic Movement." *cross talk* 4 (1975) I and II.

"On-Site Theological Training." *Christian Century* (February 5–12, 1975) 123–28.

"On Wrestling with God." *The Jewish Spectator* 40 (Spring 1975) 35–42.

El 'Don de Lenguas' en el Movimiento Carismatico, ediciones "luminar," Mexico, D.F. translated by Dr. Gonzalo Baez-Camargo.

"John the Baptist." In *Interpreter's Dictionary of the Bible, Supplementary Volume,* edited by Keith Crim, 487–88. Nashville: Abingdon, 1976.

"Symposium on Bible Criticism." *Theology Today* 33 (1977) 366.

"Wink's Study Method: A Glimpse." *Seminary Soundings* (May 1977).

"The Elements of the Universe in Biblical and Scientific Perspective." *Zygon* 13 (1978) 225–48.

"On Wrestling With God: The Use of Psychological Insights in Biblical Study." *Religion in Life* 47 (1978) 136–47.

"Unmasking the Powers." *Sojourners* 7 (October 1978) 9–15.

"Biblical Perspectives on Homosexuality." *Christian Century* (November 7, 1979) 1082–86.

"The Parable of the Compassionate Samaritan: A Communal Exegesis Approach." *Review and Expositor* 76 (1979) 199–217.

1980

"Hearing the Message." *Christianity and Crisis* (December 22, 1980) 365.

"Letting Parables Live." *Christian Century* (November 5, 1980) 1062–64.

"Where It is Lost is As Important as That It is Lost." *APCE Advocate* (May 1980) 1.

1981

"Get the Log Out!" *Baptist Leader* (September 1981).

"Loving to Hate the Moral Majority." *CALC Report* (June 1981) 2–3.

"The Preacher as Artist: An Interview with J. Phillip Swander." *The Christian Ministry* (March 1981).

1982

"The Bible in Human Transformation. An Interview with Walter Wink." *Journal of Christian Healing* 5 (1982) 33–40.
"Can You Describe the Angel of Your Church?" *Letters from the Association for Relational Christianity* (November 1982) 1.
"Faith and Nuclear Paralysis." *Christian Century* (March 3, 1982) 234–37.
"Mark 9:2–8." *Interpretation* 36 (1982) 63–67.

1983

"Matthew 4:1–11." *Interpretation* 37 (1983) 392–97.
"The Peace That Passes Understanding." *Journal for Preachers* (Easter 1983) 1–5.
"Sexual Politics in the Resurrection Witness." In *Social Themes of the Christian Year*, edited by Dieter Hessel, 177–82. Philadelphia: Geneva, 1983.

1984

"Naming the Powers." *The Auburn News* (Fall 1984).
"The Powers Behind the Throne." *Sojourners* 13 (September 1984) 22–25.

1985

"A Mind Full of Surprises." *Sojourners* 14 (December 1985) 25.
"The Purpose of Bible Study Is to Transform Us." In *Scripture: The WORD Beyond the Word*, edited by Nancy A. Carter, 21–26. New York: Women's Division, General Board of Global Ministries, The United Methodist Church, 1985.

1986

"Armed Revolution in South Africa? A Response to CALC's Covenant Against Apartheid Campaign." *CALC Report* (July/August 1986) 27–28.
"We Have Met The Enemy: On Not Becoming What We Hate." *Sojourners* 15 (November 1986) 14–18.
"Nuclear Paralysis." *Faith at Work* (June 1986) 4–5.
"The Third Way: Reclaiming Jesus' Nonviolent Alternative." *Sojourners* 15 (December 1986) 28–33.

1987

"Entering the Fire: Violence and Nonviolence in South Africa." *Sojourners* 16 (January 1987) 26–31.
"Jesus' Third Way." *International Christian Digest* (1987) 8–10.
"John the Baptist." In *The Encyclopedia of Religion*, edited by Mircea Eliade, 8:112–13. New York: Macmillan, 1987.
"My Enemy, My Destiny: The Transforming Power of Nonviolence." *Sojourners* 16 (February 1987) 30–35.

"Pacifism vs. Passivism: On Revolutionary Nonviolence." *The Sun* (August 1987) 4–12.

Review of *Jesus: The Evidence*, by Ian Wilson. *Quarterly Review* (Spring 1987) 103–8.

1988

"Educating the Apostles: Mark's View of Human Transformation." *Religious Education* 83 (1988) 277–90.

"Incarnating Holy Spirit." In *Disciplines*, 14–20. Nashville: Upper Room Press, 1988.

"Interpretation—A Retrospective." *Auburn News* (Spring 1988) 6–7.

"Neither Passivity Nor Violence: Jesus' Third Way." In *Society of Biblical Literature 1988 Seminar Papers*, edited by David Lull, 210–24. Atlanta: Scholars, 1988.

"Nonviolent Direct Action Tops the Church Agenda." *Fellowship*, September 1988, 8–9.

"Unarmed Direct Action in South Africa." *Amarillo Advocate* (July/August 1988) 11–12.

"Violence and Nonviolence in South Africa." *Dialogue and Resistance* (Winter 1987) 1–3; (Summer, 1988): 1–3.

"Walter Wink on 'Unmasking the Powers.'" *Centering* 5 (1988) 14.

1989

"Jesus' Reply to John: Matt. 11:2–6//Luke 7:18–23." *Forum* 5.1 (1989) 121–28.

Review of *Psychological Aspects of Pauline Theology*, by Gerd Theissen. *Religious Studies Review* 15 (January 1989) 40–42.

1990

"Biting the Bullet: The Case for Legalizing Drugs." *Christian Century* (August 8–15, 1990) 736–39.

"God is the Intercessor." *Sojourners* 19 (November 1990) 23–24.

Holy Week Meditations, *Disciplines*. Nashville: Upper Room Press, 1990.

"The Hymn of the Cosmic Christ." In *The Conversation Continues: Studies in Paul and John in Honor of J. Louis Martyn*, edited by Robert T. Fortna and Beverly R. Gaventa, 235–45. Nashville: Abingdon, 1990.

"Is There an Ethic of Violence?" *The Way* (April 1990) 103–13.

"Jesus' Third Way." In *The Universe Bends Towards Justice*, ed. Angie O'Gorman, 253–65. Philadelphia: New Society Publishers, 1990.

"The New RSV: The Best Translation, Halfway There." *Christian Century*, September 19–26, 1990, 829–33.

"Prayer and the Powers: History Belongs to the Intercessors." *Sojourner* 19 (October 1990) 10–14.

"Unmasking the Powers That Be." *The Door* (February 1990) 14–17.

Untitled Contributions. *Questions of Faith: Contemporary Thinkers Respond*, edited by Dolly K. Patterson. Philadelphia: Trinity Press International, 1990.

"Waging Spiritual Warfare with the Powers." *Weavings* (April 1990) 32–40.

1991

"Breaking the Spiral of Violence: The Victory of the Cross." *Bulletin of the Colloquium on Violence and Religion* (September 1991) 7.

"In the Beginning Was the Word." *APCE Advocate*, Winter 1991.

"Loving Our Enemies: The Litmus Test." *The Witness* (November 1991) 14–17.

"Neither Passivity nor Violence: Jesus' Third Way (Matt 5:38–42//Luke 6:29–30)." *Forum* 7 (1991): 5–28.

"Walking M. Scott Peck's Less-Traveled Road." *Theology Today* 48 (1991) 279–89.

1992

"All Will Be Redeemed." *The Other Side* (November–December, 1992) 16–23.

"Beyond Just War and Pacifism: Jesus' Nonviolent Way." *Review and Expositor* 89 (1992) 197–214.

"Beyond Pacifism and Just War." *Life and Peace Review* (Uppsala, Sweden) 6/2 (1992) 44–47.

"Bible Study and Movement for Human Transformation." *Body and Bible*, edited by Björn Krondorfer, 120–32. Philadelphia: Trinity, 1992.

"A Brazen Faith." *Sojourners* 21 (October 1992) 24–25.

"But What If . . . ?" *Fellowship* (April–May 1992) 20–21.

"Demons and D.Min.'s." *Review and Expositor* 89 (1992) 503–13.

"Evicted, Yet Welcomed Home." *Sojourners* 21 (June 1992) 28–29.

"The God Who Suffers and Transforms Evil." *The Living Pulpit* (October–December, 1992) 14–15.

"The Myth of Redemptive Violence." *Sojourners* 21 (April 1992) 18–21, 35.

"Neither Passivity Nor Violence: Jesus' Third Way" and "Counterresponse to Richard Horsley." In *The Love of Enemy and Nonretaliation in the New Testament*, edited by Willard M. Swartley, 102–25, 133–36. Louisville: Westminster/John Knox, 1992.

"Road Signs and Squeaky Wheels." *Sojourners* 21 (July 1992) 28–29.

"Seeking a New Thing." *Sojourners* 21 (April 1992) 28–29.

"Victory Songs and Fish Fries." *Sojourners* 21 (May 1992) 28–30.

"A World Overturned." *Sojourners* 21 (August–September 1992) 27–30.

1993

"Nonviolence in the Arena." A regular feature in *Fellowship*, co–authored with Jo Clare Hartsig. September/October, 1993 through November/December, 2005.

"Against Perfectionism." *The Witness* 76 (March 1993) 8–9.

"Babylon Revisited: How Our Violent Origins Resurface in Today's Media." *Media and Values* 62 (Spring 1993) 3–5.

"Disability and Normalcy." *Auburn Views* 1 (Spring 1993) 1–6.

"Ecobible: The Bible and Ecojustice." *Theology Today* (1993) 465–76.

"The End of Pacifism." *Evangelical Friend* 26 (March/April 1993) 14–15.

"Engaging the Powers: Discernment and Resistance in a World of Domination." 1993 Pax Christi USA Book Award Acceptance Speech. *Pax Christi USA* 18 (Winter 1993) 4–6.

"'Holy and Without Blemish Before God': Disability and Normalcy." In *And Show Steadfast Love: A Theological Look at Grace, Hospitality, Disabilities and the Church*, ed. Lewis H. Merrick, 71–82. Louisville: Presbyterian Publishing House, 1993.

"Jesus and the Nonviolent Struggle of Our Time." *Louvain Studies* 18 (Spring 1993) 3–20.

"John the Baptist." In *The Oxford Companion to the Bible*, edited by Bruce M. Metzger and Michael D. Coogan, 371–73. Oxford: Oxford University Press, 1993.

"Our Stories, Cosmic Stories, and the Biblical Story." In *Sacred Stories: A Celebration of the Power of Stories to Transform and Heal*, edited by Charles and Anne Simpkinson, 209–22. San Francisco: HarperSanFrancisco, 1993.

"The Power of the Small." *The Other Side* 29 (July–August 1993) 36–41.

Untitled Exegesis. *Lectionary Homiletics* 4 (October 1993) 1, 9, 17, 26, 34.

"Using the Bible as a Weapon against Evil." *The United Church Observer* (Canada) 56 (April 1993) 39–41.

"Waging Spiritual Warfare with the Powers." In *The Weavings Reader: Living with God in the World*, edited by John Mogabgab, 93–100. Nashville: Upper Room Books, 1993.

1994

"Against Perfectionism." *Christian* (England) 94/1 (1994) 12–13.

"Les antithèses de Matthieu: Résistance ou soumission?" *Cahiers de la réconciliation* (mouvement international de la réconciliation, Paris) 2 (1994) 12–15.

"Appreciating Gnosticism." *Dialog* 33 (1994) 99–105.

"Beat the System." *Third Way* (Middlesex, England) 17 (December 1994) 17–18.

"The Bible and Exclusion, Bias and Prejudice." *The Witness* 77 (June 1994) 14–16.

"Engaging the Powers: Discernment and Resistance in a World of Domination." *Radical Grace* 7 (April–May 1994) 9.

"The Gospel and Conflict." *Living Pulpit* (July–September 1994) 14–15.

"Jesus Never Said 'Be Perfect.'" *Response* 26 (February 1994) 13–17.

"A Man to Match His Mountains: Badshah Khan, Nonviolent Soldier of Islam." *Fellowship* 60 (May/June 1994) 28.

"Nonviolence Does Work." In *World Without Violence*, edited by Arun Gandhi, 248–49. New Delhi: Wiley Eastern Limited, 1994.

"Nonviolence in the Arena." A regular feature in *Fellowship*, co-authored with Jo Clare Hartsig. September/October, 1993 through November/December, 2005.

Series in *Christian Century*:

"Resonating with God's Song." *Christian Century* (March 23–30) 1994, 309.

"Chips Off the Old Block." *Christian Century* (April 6, 1994) 349.

"Those Obstreperous Idiots." *Christian Century* (April 13, 1994) 381.

"Abiding, Even Under the Knife." *Christian Century* (April 20, 1994) 413.

"The Other World Is Here." *Christian Century* (April 27, 1994) 443.

"Armed With Truth." *Christian Century* (May 4, 1994) 465.

"These Bones Shall Live." *Christian Century* (May 11, 1994) 491.

"Messianic Complex." *Christian Century* (May 18–25, 1994) 523.

"The Projector Is Running." *Christian Century* (June 1–8, 1994) 571.

"Real, At Any Cost." *Christian Century* (June 15–22, 1994) 603.

"Toying with Violence." *The Witness* (December 1994) 6.

"Write What You See: An Autobiographical Reflection." *Fourth R* 7 (May/June 1994) 3–9.

1995

"Beyond Just War and Pacifism." In *War and Its Discontents: Pacifism and Quietism in the Western Monotheisms,* edited by J. Patout Burns, 102–21. Washington, DC: Georgetown University Press, 1995.

"Biblical Theology and Social Ethics." *Biblical Theology: Problems and Perspectives: In Honor of J. Christiaan Beker,* edited by Stephen J. Kraftchick, Charles D. Myers, Jr., and Ben C. Ollenburger, 260–75. Nashville: Abingdon, 1995.

"The Kingdom: God's Domination-Free Order." In *Communion, Community, Commonweal: Readings for Spiritual Leadership,* edited by John S. Mogabgab, 157–65. Nashville: Upper Room Books, 1995.

"The Kingdom: God's Domination-free Order." *Weavings* 10 (January/February 1995) 6–15.

"Is Marriage God-Ordained?" *The Witness* (December 1995) 12.

"Nonviolence in the Arena." A regular feature in *Fellowship,* co-authored with Jo Clare Hartsig. September/October, 1993 through November/December, 2005.

"The Powers Made Us Do It." *Christian Century* (November 1, 1995) 117–18.

"Principalities and Powers: A Different Worldview." *Church and Society* (May/June 1995) 18–28.

Review of "Not the Way It's Supposed to Be," by Cornelius Plantinga, Jr. *Christian Century* (November 1, 1995) 117–18.

"Standing on the Rock of the Impossible" and "'Normalcy' as Disease: Facing Disabilities." *Church and Society* (May/June 1995) 3–17.

"Stringfellow on the Powers." In *Radical Christian and Exemplary Lawyer,* edited by Andrew W. McThenia, Jr., 17–30. Grand Rapids: Eerdmans, 1995.

"William Stringfellow: Theologian of the Next Millennium." *CrossCurrents* 45 (Summer 1995) 205–16.

1996

"A Conversation with Walter Wink." *Alive Now* (November/December 1996) 24–29.

"Dan Berrigan as Theologian." In *Apostle of Peace: Essays in Honor of Daniel Berrigan,* edited by John Dear, 77–80. Maryknoll, NY: Orbis, 1996.

"El Reino, un Sistema Libre de Dominación de Dios." *Extus: Espiritu Y Cultura* (Mexico) 4/17 (1996) 4–11.

"Getting Off Drugs." *Friends Journal* 42 (February 1996) 13–16.

"The Gospel and Work." *The Living Pulpit* (July–September 1996) 8–9.

"Healing a Nation's Wounds." *New Routes* 1 (Spring, 1996) 13–16.

"Homosexuality and the Bible." Nyack, NY: Fellowship Publications, 1996; revised and updated, 2005. (Available from Fellowship of Reconciliation, Box 271, Nyack, NY 10960, and online at www.forusa.org.)

"Nonviolence in the Arena." A regular feature in *Fellowship,* co-authored with Jo Clare Hartsig. September/October, 1993 through November/December, 2005.

Review of *Violence Unveiled,* by Gil Bailie. *Pax Christi USA* 21 (1996).

"What?! Did He Say 'Tithe'?!" *The Witness* (December 1996) 20–22.

1997

"The Apocalyptic Beast: The Culture of Violence." *Concilium* 1997 no. 5, "The Return of the Plague," 71–77.

"Getting Off Drugs: A Nonviolent Alternative to the Drug War." *Fellowship* (January/February 1997) 4.

"The Holocaust at Home." *Ministry of Money* (August 1997) 1–2.

"Homosexuality and the Bible." *Fellowship* (March/April 1997) 12–15.

"Incarnating the Spirit." *Upper Room Disciplines 1997*, 157–63. Nashville: Upper Room Books, 1997.

Introduction to *Voices of the Voiceless*, by Michelle Tooley. Scottdale, PA: Herald, 1997.

"Nonviolence in the Arena." A regular feature in *Fellowship*, co-authored with Jo Clare Hartsig. September/October, 1993 through November/December, 2005.

"Response to Luke Timothy Johnson's *The Real Jesus*." *Bulletin for Biblical Research* 7 (1997) 233–48.

"You Give Them Something to Eat." *Bread* (Bread for the World Newsletter) (9 May 1997) 6.

1998

"Evil in *A Wind in the Door*." In *The Swiftly Tilting Worlds of Madeleine L'Engle*, edited by Luci Shaw. Festschrift for Madeleine L'Engle, 27–35. Wheaton, IL: Shaw, 1998.

"Going the Second Mile." *The Witness* (July/August 1998) 14.

"The Humanchild." *Radical Grace* (April/May 1998) 12.

"Jesus' Third Way." In *Transforming Nonviolence*, edited by Robert Herr and Judy Zimmerman Herr, 34–47. Scottdale, PA: Herald, 1998.

"Nonviolence in the Arena." A regular feature in *Fellowship*, co-authored with Jo Clare Hartsig. September/October, 1993 through November/December, 2005.

1999

"Celebrating the Guild's Founders." *Intersection: Journal of the Guild for Psychological Studies* (1999) 14–27.

"Drug Policy: The Fix We're In." *Christian Century* (February 24, 1999) 214–17.

"Getting Off Drugs: A Nonviolent Alternative to the Drug War." *Ka'u Landing* (February 1999) 35–37.

"The Gladsome Doctrine of Sin." *The Living Pulpit* (October–December 1999) 4–5.

"Guest Editorial: A Call to Nonviolent Direct Action." *Interconnect* (May 1999) 2.

"Nonviolence in the Arena." A regular feature in *Fellowship*, co-authored with Jo Clare Hartsig. September/October, 1993 through November/December, 2005.

"Reconciliation." In *Encyclopedia of Violence, Peace and Conflict*, edited by Lester Kurtz. San Diego: Academic Press, 1999.

"The Spirits of Institutions." In *The Hidden Spirit: Discovering the Spirituality of Institutions*, edited by James F. Cobble, Jr. and Charles M. Elliott, 16–24. Matthews, NC: Christian Ministry Resources, 1999.

"A Theologian on Kosovo: What is the Response of Nonviolence?" *The Messenger* (May 1999) 16–19.
"A Time to Weep." *Sojourners* 28 (July–August 1999) 21.

2000

"Nonviolence in the Arena." A regular feature in *Fellowship,* co-authored with Jo Clare Hartsig. September/October, 1993 through November/December, 2005.
"The Redeeming Power of the Small." *Fellowship* (January–February 2000) 4.
"The Son of Man: The Stone That the Builders Rejected." In *The Once and Future Jesus,* by Robert Funk et. al., 161–80. Santa Rosa, CA: Polebridge, 2000.
"Without a Vision the People Perish." *The Other Side* (March/April 2000) 10–13.

2001

"Apocalypse Now?" *Christian Century* (October 17, 2001) 16–19.
Forward to *Walking Jesus' Path of Peace,* by Rosalyn Falcon Collier, et. al. Minneapolis: Augsburg Fortress Press, 2001.
"Guns R Us?" *Christian Century* (March 21–28, 2001) 21–29.
"Left Reeling." *The Lutheran* 14 (November 2001) 18–19.
"Nonviolence for the Violent." *The Fourth R* 14 (September/October 2001) 3–5.
"Nonviolence in the Arena." A regular feature in *Fellowship,* co-authored with Jo Clare Hartsig. September/October, 1993 through November/December, 2005.
"The Silence of God." *Sojourners* (November/December 2001) 28.
"Which Worldview Do You Choose?" *Connections* 103 (May 2001) 1–4.

2002

"Christianity's Gift," *Sojourners* 31 (March/April 2002) 57.
"Edifying Tales of Nonviolence." *Radical Grace* (April–June 2002) 3–5.
"Gays and the Bible." *Christian Century* (August 14–27, 2002) 40–44.
"Loving Our Enemies." In *Ashes Transformed,* edited by Tilda Norberg, 174–78. Nashville: Upper Room Books, 2002.
"Nonviolence in the Arena." A regular feature in *Fellowship,* co-authored with Jo Clare Hartsig. September/October, 1993 through November/December, 2005.
"Strength for Our Times." In *Upper Room Disciplines 2002,* 342–55. Nashville: Upper Room Books, 2002.
"To Hell with Gays?" *Christian Century* (June 5–12, 2002) 32–34.
"The Wrong Apocalypse." In *In The Aftermath: What September 11th is Teaching us about Our World, Our Faith and Ourselves,* edited by James Taylor. Kelowna, BC, Canada: Northstone Publishing, 2002.
"Pacifism with Teeth." *Yes! A Journal of Positive Futures* (Winter 2002) 13–15.

2003

"An Appreciation of Hal Childs' Critique of Historical Jesus Research." *Pastoral Psychology* 51 (2003) 481–86.

"Can Love Save the World?" In *Making Peace*, edited by Carolyn McConnell and Sarah Ruth van Gelder, 46–50. Bainbridge Island, WA: Positive Futures Network, 2003.

"Fannie Lou Hamer: Baptism by Fire." *Fellowship* (September/October 2003) 25.

"The Next Worldview: Spirit at the Core of Everything." *Fellowship* (May/June 2003) 6–11.

"Nonviolence in the Arena." A regular feature in *Fellowship,* co-authored with Jo Clare Hartsig. September/October, 1993 through November/December, 2005.

"Six Critics Review Walter Wink's *The Human Being: Jesus and the Enigma of the Son of The Man* (with responses by Walter Wink to each)." *Cross Currents* 53 (2003) 264–317.

"We have met the evil empire and it is us." *Berkshire Eagle* (August 6, 2003) 8.

2004

"Between Just War and Pacifism: Jesus' Nonviolent Way." In *The Destructive Power of Religion,* vol. 4, edited by J. Harold Ellens. Westport, CT: Praeger, 2004.

"Globalization and Empire." *Mississippi Review* 10 (Winter 2004) 24–39.

"Jesus and Alinsky." In *The Impossible Will Take a Little While: A Citizen's Guide to Hope in a Time of Fear,* edited by Paul Rogat Loeb, 149–60. New York: Basic Books, 2004.

"The Myth of Redemptive Violence." In *The Destructive Power of Religion,* vol. 3, ed. J. Harold Ellens, 265–86. Westport, CT: Praeger, 2004.

"Nonviolence and Globalization: Episodes." *Fellowship* (July/August 2004) 23.

"Nonviolence in the Arena." A regular feature in *Fellowship,* co-authored with Jo Clare Hartsig. September/October, 1993 through November/December, 2005.

"On Homosexual Marriage." *Christian Networks Journal* (Summer 2004) 44–45.

"Snagged by the Seat of My Pants While Reading the Bible" and "The Original Impulse of Jesus." In *Psychology and the Bible,* vol. 3, ed. J. Harold Ellens and Wayne G. Rollins, 19–28, 209–21. Westport, CT: Praeger, 2004.

Untitled Reflection. In *Hunger for the Word: Lectionary Reflections on Food and Justice, Year A,* edited by Larry Hollar, 179–200. Collegeville, MN: Liturgical, 2004.

"Wrestling with God: Psychological Insights in Biblical Study." In *Psychology and the Bible,* vol. 2, ed. J. Harold Ellens and Wayne G. Rollins, 9–22. Westport, CT: Praeger, 2004.

2005

"Globalization and Empire: We Have Met the Evil Empire and It is Us." *Political Theology* 5 (2004) 295–306.

"Nonviolence in the Arena." A regular feature in *Fellowship,* co-authored with Jo Clare Hartsig. September/October, 1993 through November/December, 2005.

Untitled prayer. *Fellowship* (May/June 2005) inside back cover.

Additional Works Cited

Anderson, Bernhard W. *Understanding the Old Testament.* 4th ed. Englewood Cliffs, NJ: Prentice-Hall, 1986.

Baille, Gil. *Violence Unveiled: Humanity at the Crossroads.* New York: Crossroads, 1995.

Barth, Karl. *The Epistle to the Romans.* Translated by Edwyn C. Hoskyns. Oxford: Oxford University Press, 1953.

Berger, Peter L. *The Sacred Canopy: Elements of a Sociological Theory of Religion.* Garden City, NY: Doubleday, 1967.

Berry, Wendell. "Manifesto: The Mad Farmer Liberation Front." In *The Country of Marriage.* New York: Harcourt Brace Jovanovich, 1973.

Boggs, Grace Lee. *Living for Change: An Autobiography.* Minneapolis: University of Minnesota Press, 1998.

Borg, Marcus. *Meeting Jesus Again for the First Time: the Historical Jesus and the Heart of Contemporary Faith.* San Francisco: HarperSanFrancisco, 1995.

Borsch, Frederick. *The Son of Man in Myth and History.* 1967. Reprinted, Eugene, OR: Wipf & Stock, 2007.

Brock, Rita Nakashima, and Rebecca Parker. *Proverbs of Ashes: Violence, Redemptive Suffering, and the Search for What Saves Us.* Boston: Beacon, 2001.

Brown, Raymond E. *The Death of the Messiah: From Gethsemane to the Grave. A Commentary on the Passion in the Four Gospels.* New York: Doubleday, 1994.

Bultmann, Rudolf. *The History of the Synoptic Tradition.* Translated by John Marsh. Oxford: Blackwell, 1963.

Calvin, John. *Institutes of the Christian Religion.* Translated by Ford Lewis Battles. Edited by John T. McNeill. Philadelphia: Westminster, 1960.

Campbell, Charles L. *The Word before the Powers: An Ethic of Preaching.* Louisville: Westminster John Knox, 2002.

Childs, Hal. *The Myth of the Historical Jesus and the Evolution of Consciousness.* SBL Dissertation Series 179. Atlanta: Society of Biblical Literature, 2000.

Crossan, John Dominic. *Jesus: A Revolutionary Biography.* San Francisco: HarperSanFrancisco, 1994.

Deats, Richard. *Mahatma Gandhi: A Biography.* Hyde Park, NY: New City, 2005.

Ellens, J. Harold, Gabrielle Boccaccini, Delbert Burkett, Jack Miles, Wayne Rollins, Alan Segal and Walter Wink. "Six Critics Review Walter Wink's *The Human Being: Jesus and the Enigma of the Son of the Man.*" *Cross Currents* 53 (2003) 264–317.

Gingerich, Ray, and Ted Grimsrud, editors. *Transforming the Powers: Peace, Justice and the Domination System.* Minneapolis: Fortress, 2006.

Gorringe, Timothy. *God's Just Vengeance: Crime, Violence and the Rhetoric of Salvation.* New York: Cambridge University Press, 1996.

Habermas, Jürgen. *Knowledge and Human Interests.* Translated by J. J. Shapiro. Boston: Beacon, 1971.

Hauerwas, Stanley. *The Peaceable Kingdom: A Primer in Christian Ethics.* Notre Dame: University of Notre Dame Press, 1983.

Hall, Douglas John. *The End of Christendom and the Future of Christianity.* 1996. Reprinted, Eugene, OR: Wipf & Stock, 2002.

Inter-Lutheran Commission on Worship. *The Lutheran Book of Worship.* Minneapolis: Augsburg, 1978.

Jacobsen, Dennis. *Doing Justice: Congregations and Community Organizing.* Minneapolis: Fortress, 2001.

Jung, Carl Gustav. *The Collected Works of C. G. Jung.* Translated by R. F. C. Hull. Edited by Gerhard Adler. 20 vols. Bollingen Series. Princeton: Princeton University, 1953–78.

Kaufman, Gordon. *In Face of Mystery: A Constructive Theology.* Cambridge: Harvard University Press, 1993.

Kraybill, Ronald S., Robert A. Evans, and Alice Frazer Evans. *Peace Skills Set: Manual for Community Mediators. Leaders' Guide.* San Francisco: Jossey-Bass, 2001.

Kuhn, Thomas S. *The Structure of Scientific Revolutions.* 2d ed. Chicago: University of Chicago Press, 1970.

Laffin, Arthur, and Anne Montgomery, editors. *Swords Into Plowshares: Nonviolent Direct Action for Disarmament.* New York: Harper & Row, 1987.

LaHaye, Timothy, and Jerry B. Jenkins. *The Left Behind Book Series.* Books 1–13. Wheaton, IL: Tyndale, 2000–2007.

Lindsey, Hal, and Carol Carlson. *The Late Great Planet Earth.* Grand Rapids: Zondervan, 1970.

Marshall, Christopher. *Beyond Retribution: A New Testament Vision for Justice, Crime and Punishment.* Grand Rapids: Eerdmans, 2001.

McClain, George. *Claiming All Things for God: Prayer, Discernment, and Ritual for Social Change.* Nashville: Abingdon, 1998.

McIntosh, Alastair. *Soil and Soul: People versus Corporate Power.* 3rd ed. London: Aurum Press, 2004.

Mega, Marcello. "Cigarette Ads may Induce Death Wish." *Sunday Times,* August 8, 1996, Scottish edition, 10.

Nelson-Pallmeyer, Jack. *Jesus Against Christianity: Reclaiming the Missing Jesus.* Harrisburg, PA: Trinity, 2001.

"The Order of D. F. Strauss." *The Fourth R* 12.5–6 (1999) 27.

Pannenberg, Wolfhart. *Systematic Theology.* Vol. 1. Translated by Geoffrey W. Bromiley. Grand Rapids: Eerdmans, 1991.

Parker-Pope, Tara. "No Butts About It: British Tobacco Ads Keep Burning Bright." *Wall Street Journal,* October 10, 1996, European edition, sec 1.

Rilke, Rainer Maria. *Letters to a Young Poet.* Translated by M. D. Herter Norton. New York: Norton, 1934.

Saunders, Stanley P., and Charles Campbell. *The Word on the Street.* 2000. Reprinted, Eugene, OR: Wipf & Stock, 2007.

Schleiermacher, Friedrich. *The Christian Faith.* Trans. H. R. Mackintosh and J. S. Stewart. Edinburgh: T. & T. Clark, 1999.

Schweitzer, Albert. *The Quest of the Historical Jesus, A Critical Study of its Progress From Reimarus to Wrede.* New York: Macmillan, 1968.

Seiple, D. Review of Walter Wink, *The Human Being: Jesus and the Enigma of the Son of Man. Union Seminary Quarterly Review* 55.3–4 (2001) 178–83.

Smith, Wilfred Cantwell. *Toward a World Theology: Faith and the Comparative History of Religion.* Philadelphia: Westminster, 1981.

Smith, Morton. *Jesus the Magician.* San Francisco: Harper & Row, 1978.

Steiner, George. *The Idea of Europe.* Introductory essay by Rob Riemen. Tilburg, The Netherlands: Nexus Institute, 2004.

Tutu, Desmond. *God Has a Dream: A Vision of Hope for Our Time.* New York: Doubleday, 2004.

Walker, Aaron Thibeaux. "Call it Stormy Monday." First recorded on *T-Bone Walker: Low-Down Blues.* Los Angeles: Black and White Records, 1947.

Weaver, J. Denny. *The Nonviolent Atonement.* Grand Rapids: Eerdmans, 2001.

Wylie-Kellerman, Bill. "Discerning the Angel of Detroit." *Sojourners* 18 (October, 1989) 16–21.

———. *Seasons of Faith and Conscience: Kairos, Confession, Liturgy.* Maryknoll, NY: Orbis, 1991.

Yoder, John Howard. *The Politics of Jesus: Vicit Agnus Noster.* Grand Rapids: Eerdmans, 1972.

Zehr, Howard. *Changing Lenses: A New Focus for Crime and Justice.* Scottdale, PA: Herald, 1990.